TO THE TOP

THE STORY OF EVEREST

TO THE TOP

THE STORY OF EVEREST

by Stephen Venables

WALKER BOOKS

AND SUBSIDIARIES

LONDON • BOSTON • SYDNEY

PHOTOGRAPHS
Robert Anderson: 81. **Chris Bonington Picture Library:** Chris Bonington 64bm & b, 90; Leo Dickinson endpapers, 64tm, 72, 86–88, 93; Doug Scott 65, 68–70. **John Cleare/Mountain Camera Picture Library:** 89. **Hedgehog House:** Chris Curry 92. **National Geographic Image Collection:** 64t. **John Noel Photographic Collection:** 9. **Reinhold Messner:** 74. **Royal Geographical Society, London:** 2, 8, 12–13, 16–24, 27–30, 32–35, 37–40, 42–44, 46–47, 49–51, 54–58, 60–61, 63. **Paul Teare:** 77. **Willi Unsoeld** and used with permission of Jolene Unsoeld: 67. **Stephen Venables:** 6, 78–79, 82–83, 85. **Ed Webster:** 5, 75, 76, 79b.
ILLUSTRATIONS
Mike Bostock: 10–11.
CREDITS
Edited by **Paul Harrison**. Designed by **Beth Aves**.

The publisher and author are grateful to the Royal Geographical Society (with the Institute of British Geographers) for permission to use its name and logo in association with this book.

First published 2003 by Walker Books Ltd
87 Vauxhall Walk, London SE11 5HJ

1 2 3 4 5 6 7 8 9 10

Text © 2003 Stephen Venables
Illustrations © 2003 Walker Books Ltd

The right of Stephen Venables to be identified as author of this work has been asserted by him in accordance with the Copyright, Designs and Patents Act 1988

This book has been typeset in AT Arta

Printed in Singapore

ISBN 0-7445-8662-3

CONTENTS

For

Ollie and Edmond

INTRODUCTION

It was FIVE O'CLOCK in the afternoon when the shrieking wind began to quieten down and we made our decision: tonight we would leave for the summit. After weeks of hard work we had reached our top camp on Everest – 7,900 metres above sea-level. Ed Webster and I were squeezed into a tent no bigger than a single bed, with only just enough headroom to sit up. Robert Anderson had just walked over from the second tiny dome tent, but our fourth companion, Paul Teare, had left us that morning – returning down the mountain because of a worrying headache. It had been a brave decision to give up his chance at the summit, but he knew that high-altitude sickness can kill if you stay up high too long. At the top of Everest there is no chance of a rescue, so he had returned to the safety of the valley to recover. That left three of us preparing for the great day ahead.

First we had to eat and drink. At that height everything is frozen, so Ed fed chunks of crusty snow into a pan on our gas stove to make water. After about an hour the water was boiling, but at nowhere near the usual temperature: at this altitude Ed could stick his bare finger in the water without pain. This meant that cooking was out of the question, so he just stirred some instant noodles into the tepid liquid – our last proper meal for many hours. The most important thing of all at altitude is to have enough to drink, so we melted more snow, lump by lump, eventually filling two bottles, adding powdered energy

The final camp below the summit

drink to keep us going during the long day ahead.

We were leaving at night. The idea was to reach the summit by early afternoon the next day and regain our tents by nightfall. However, if the worst came to the worst and we failed to return in time, I wanted to be sure I could survive a night out in the open, so I took great care with my many layers of clothing.

I was already wearing thermal underwear, socks, a fleece suit and a second fleece jacket, plus chest-high trousers padded thickly with finest goose down. Now I added my down jacket, pulling its hood over two balaclavas to insulate my head. Over

Robert Anderson summons the strength to put on crampons

the top of the whole lot I pulled a one-piece suit of windproof material. The water bottle went into an inner pocket, close to my body, to stop it freezing.

Then it was time to sort out my feet. First I pulled foam inner boots over my socks, then stiff plastic outer boots, rather like ski boots, which I had been keeping warm in my sleeping-bag. Then, panting with the effort and stopping frequently to rest, I pulled on over boots – giant zip-up socks of wetsuit material reaching to the knee. Before crawling out of the tent, I pulled goose-down mittens over my inner gloves, then fleece and windproof mittens over the top of them. Sunglasses were stowed in a pocket for later; I'd already smeared a thick layer of suncream all over my face.

The final task before leaving was to fit crampons – steel spikes which clip onto your boots – for a firm grip on snow and ice. Even at sea-level this is quite a fiddly job. Here, 7,900 metres higher, it was desperate. There is less than half the air pressure there is at sea-level; and at the summit – which is about the height that jet aeroplanes fly – there would only be one third, as the higher you go the less pressure there is. This means that it's incredibly hard to get enough oxygen into your lungs and even the smallest task takes your breath away. I gasped and struggled hopelessly. And then there was the cold. To handle the fiddly crampon clips, I had to remove my mittens – but at -30°C, the steel quickly numbed my fingers, and I had to keep getting back into the tent to blow my hands back to life.

At last, at 11.00 p.m., we were ready. There was no moon, but the sky was brilliant with stars and there wasn't a breath of wind – a perfect night for the job. Above us the snow made pale patterns on the dark rock. Even at night we could just make out enough landmarks to know roughly where to go. Each of us had a torch strapped to his head and carried an ice axe, which is like a walking-stick with a sharp steel pick at the top end. Joining the three of us was a short length of nylon rope. If someone slipped, the other two would try to hold him on the rope.

We started to plod very slowly towards the summit, knowing the journey would take at least twelve hours. At first it was flat and we could manage twenty paces before we had to stop and rest. But as the slope steepened, and we had to kick steps into the frozen snow crust, we were forced to stop every ten paces – taking two, maybe three, deep breaths to each one. At times it felt as though someone was holding a wet flannel over your face. I had never worked so hard in my life.

But despite all that, I was thrilled to be there. Looking down, I could see that we were slowly gaining height. Our tents were now two tiny dark dots on the gleaming snow, far below. Midnight had passed and soon it would be dawn. I hardly dared to hope for it, but if we were lucky, today would be the day we climbed to the very top of the world.

Before I finish my story, I need to tell you about the earliest attempts to find a way up Everest. But first we should look at the mountain itself. What is it like, this giant, and how did it get there in the first place?

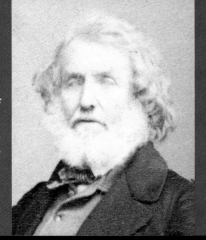

Left: Sir George Everest, Director of the Survey of India, after whom Everest was named

Right: the start of Everest's gigantic North-east Ridge

THE MYSTERY OF EVEREST

"One mountain in particular fascinated
the surveyors. They did not know that it
had a local name, Chomolungma,
so they called it 'Peak XV.'"

1

Many PEOPLE IMAGINE that Everest is a single great peak, rising all alone above an empty flat plain. After all, some mountains, such as Africa's Kilimanjaro, are like that. But Everest is not. It is just one of literally thousands and thousands of mountains that make up the range called Himalaya.

The Himalaya is the greatest range on earth, yet as mountain ranges go it is quite young, formed about 50 million years ago. The surface of the earth is split into pieces of rock, called plates. These plates are constantly on the move, although only very slowly — a few millimetres a year. This movement is known as plate tectonics. If two plates bump into each other the edges can crumple up over time and form mountains. This is how the Himalaya was formed.

Some rocks were buried deep beneath the earth. They were squeezed and melted to form granite, which then bubbled back to the surface. This pale granite, only about 20 million years old, can be seen near the base of Everest. But some of the oldest rocks rode high above

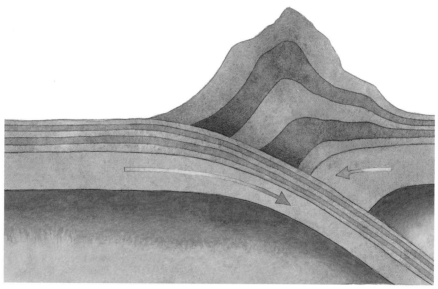

A cross-section showing mountain formation as a result of plate movement. The arrows show the directions the two plates are moving in. The mountains form where the two plates collide.

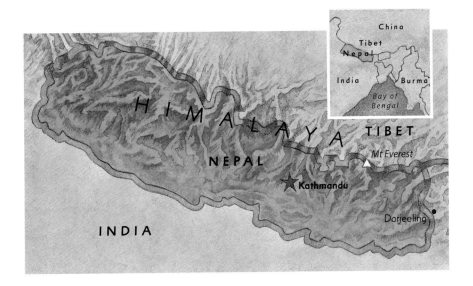

all the chaos, completely unchanged. Close to the summit of Everest there is a layer of limestone, the "Yellow Band", which was originally formed from the remains of crushed sea-creatures. Those rocks started life on the bottom of an ancient ocean called the Tethys Sea, about 480 million years ago.

Although the Himalayan range lies close to the warm tropics, even there, as you climb higher into the earth's atmosphere, the air becomes cooler. Above 5,000 metres most Himalayan peaks are covered in snow all the year round. In winter the snow falls much further down the mountain. There are the glaciers, too — slow-moving rivers of ice left over from the ice ages. They generally flow down to altitudes of about 4,000 metres above sea-level, but some are found at 3,000 metres.

Looking from India, to the south, the range seems like a dazzling white curtain in the sky. The name "Himalaya" is an old Indian word meaning "abode of snow". Long before Europeans arrived in India, the mountains were simply a source of wonder for generations of Hindus. The permanent snows were not just beautiful; they melted to feed the rivers which were necessary for the survival of the people below. Because the mountains are so impossibly high, glittering and remote — and the source of life itself — many summits are considered holy in Hinduism and Buddhism. Many of the people who actually live among the Himalayan peaks are Buddhists. The head of their religion is the Dalai Lama, who until recently was also the ruler of Tibet, the huge country on the north side of the Himalaya. For many years Buddhist

11

Rongbuk Monastery with Everest in the background

holy men lived alone in caves right beneath Everest itself, until a monastery was built at Rongbuk in 1902, 4,800 metres above sea-level and just a few kilometres from the earth's highest summit.

To the monks at Rongbuk – and to all the villagers and nomadic shepherds living near by – the great mountain we call Everest was always known as "Chomolungma". No one is sure what the name means. Some scholars say it means "peak above the valley"; others think it is "great bird in the sky", or "mother goddess of the earth". Whatever its precise meaning, for Tibetans and their southern neighbours many rivers, lakes, mountains, passes and cliffs have always been sacred.

Then the Europeans came to India. The Portuguese explorer Vasco da Gama arrived at India in 1498 and within a few years Portuguese traders were settling there, followed quickly by the British, who gradually took control. By the nineteenth century India had become part of the British Empire, and British surveyors began the gigantic task of mapping the entire Indian subcontinent. Eventually they reached the great barrier to the north – the Himalaya. The range stretches over 2,400 kilometres, from Afghanistan in the west to China and Burma in he east. In places the barrier is up to 480 kilometres across. Many of the thousands of peaks are in India, but some of the highest lie in Nepal and many, like Everest, are found on the frontier between Nepal and Tibet.

Until recently no foreigners were allowed into either of these countries. For the British map-makers in the nineteenth century this made things very difficult. To get round this problem, they trained Indian map-makers to enter Tibet illegally, disguised as Buddhist pilgrims. These "pundits", as they were called, made long and dangerous journeys to bring back much useful information.

Most of the work was done from a distance in India, however, using special optical instruments to make sense of the distant bumps around 100 kilometres away on the horizon. One mountain in particular fascinated the surveyors. They did not know that it had a local name, Chomolungma, so they called it "Peak XV". In 1854, after checking all their complicated calculations, they declared that this was the highest summit on earth. According to their measurements it was 8,839.8 metres above the distant ocean. Later, after more measuring, it was given a height of 8,848 metres above sea-level. Finally, in 2001, using laser equipment, modern surveyors announced a new height of 8,849.646 metres above sea-level. (In fact the mountain is still growing, though only by a few millimetres a year.)

It seems that the British and Indian surveyors in the nineteenth century were just about spot-on. Thrilled to have discovered the highest mountain on earth they decided that Peak XV needed a name. Unaware of its correct Tibetan name, they decided to call it after one of the men who had led the whole gigantic project of mapping the Indian subcontinent – Sir George Everest.

Although no European had set foot on Everest, over 8,000 kilometres away in Europe people were beginning to explore the peaks of another range – the Alps; the pastime of mountaineering was starting to take off. Most people were puzzled about why anyone would want to risk their life on a dangerous precipice – and that is still true today, even though mountaineering is more popular.

There is no easy explanation. For me there are many attractions. There is the gymnastic thrill of balancing up steep cliffs; tightrope-walking along the knife-edge crest of a ridge, high in the sky. There is the colour and shape of the rocks, the glitter of snow and ice; the enjoyment of being outdoors, climbing high above the earth, sleeping out under the stars, treading high above the clouds. It is almost as if you have entered a different, magical world.

Of course there are also dangers. Thin bridges of snow sometimes hide crevasses – deep splits in the glacier ice beneath the snow. Towers of ice can collapse, crushing anyone caught beneath them. Loose rocks can tumble down the mountain or thousands of tonnes of snow can come crashing down in an avalanche. In extreme cold there is the risk of frostbite, which can mean losing fingers or toes. On the very highest mountains, starved of oxygen, you can get high-altitude sickness. And any mistake above a huge drop could result in you falling to your death. It takes skill, experience and special equipment to cope with these dangers. The trick is to know the dangers and stay in control. Nevertheless, you can never make the danger go away completely.

For the first mountaineers the reward was to reach Alpine summits, where no human had ever trod before. By the end of the nineteenth century most of Europe's summits — and many in North America — had been climbed. Mountaineers began to wonder about the much higher peaks of the Himalaya. In 1902 a team attempted the world's second highest mountain, K2, which lies about 1,200 kilometres north-west of Everest in what is now northern Kashmir. They barely got onto the foot of the mountain. It was the same when they tried Kangchenjunga, the world's third highest mountain, in the state of Sikkim. Compared to Europe, everything in the Himalaya was gigantic, and this meant problems with altitude.

The highest summit in the Alps, Mont Blanc (on the French–Italian border) is 4,807 metres above sea-level. At that height the air is already very thin, with only half the normal pressure. But on the biggest Himalayan peaks, the hard climbing only starts at that altitude. At first no one knew whether it would be possible to survive on the highest summits, where there is even less oxygen to breathe. However, in 1909 some Italian climbers reached an altitude of 7,500 metres above sea-level on a peak near K2. Perhaps the highest summits were possible. Even Everest.

Unlike K2 and Kangchenjunga, Everest lay behind closed doors. The British, however, did have a slim chance of getting to the Tibetan side: in 1904 the British Government signed a treaty with the Dalai Lama and soon afterwards government officials asked about the possibility of sending an expedition to Everest. But before anything could happen, the First World War (1914–18) put an end to all thoughts of exploration.

Many of Britain's best young climbers were killed on the battlefields of Europe, but after the war some of the older members of the Alpine Club and the Royal Geographical Society tried again to organize an expedition to Tibet. Finally, in 1921, the Dalai Lama issued a special passport allowing a team of British explorers to enter his country and visit the mountain he called Chomolungma. The 1921 expedition set sail for Asia — the long journey to Everest's summit had finally begun.

Below: the 1921
Advance Base Camp
on the north-east
side of Everest

Above: George
Mallory

Right: Guy Bullock
and some porters
try out snowshoes
for the first time

UNLOCKING THE SECRETS

"To some mountaineers this solving of
a puzzle is more exciting than
attempting the summit."

2

When I WENT TO CLIMB Everest in 1988, it took just a few hours to fly the 8,000 kilometres from London to Nepal, which is now open to foreigners. Then it was a two-day drive to Tibet, followed by a 50-kilometre walk to our camp at the foot of the mountain.

In 1921 it was utterly different. First there was a month's sea voyage to India. Then a long train journey to Darjeeling. This town, famous for its tea gardens, is perched on the side of a hill just to the south of the Himalaya. On a fine day you can just see Everest from here. But you still have to travel 400 kilometres to get there – and in 1921 there was no road. The whole journey had to be done on foot. Everything – food, cooking fuel, stoves, climbing equipment, tents and sleeping-bags – had to be carried on the backs of either human porters or pack animals.

In addition, the expedition had to carry theodolites (for measuring angles and distances), telescopes, compasses and plane-tables (portable drawing boards for recording findings), as well as paper, pencil and pens – all the equipment used for making a map. This was because in 1921 there was no map of Everest.

Photograph of an overnight camp on the long journey to Tibet, taken in 1924

That is why the expedition was called the Everest Reconnaissance. They were not going to climb the mountain; they were going to find the way to the bottom and see if there might be a possible route to the summit.

So the team of eight British explorers set off from Darjeeling, accompanied by a great caravan of porters, pack animals, interpreters and guides. First they had to drop right down to the Teesta River — barely 700 metres above sea-level — and into the steaming heat of the jungle. Only gradually did they climb up through the jungle, right up into the Himalaya and, eventually, across a high pass into Tibet.

Tibet is a huge place, the size of France and Germany combined. It is the highest country on earth — an immense plateau stretching north from the Himalaya. On a fine day it is very beautiful. The air is clear and bright, the rolling hills are gold, red and purple and the lakes are a brilliant turquoise. But it is also a dry, dusty, windy place and at times it feels very bleak. In 1921 it must have seemed doubly depressing when the oldest member of the team, 52-year-old Dr Alexander Kellas, became ill with dysentery and died.

Poor Kellas was buried at a remote, desolate grave and the others continued sadly towards Everest. Most of them were not climbers as such — more general explorers with some mountain experience. Using plane-tables and theodolites, Henry Morshead and Oliver Wheeler surveyed the land they travelled through, producing the first ever map of the Everest region. The leader, Charles Howard-Bury, took many of the magnificent photographs that now live at the Royal Geographical Society in London. As for finding an actual climbing route up the mountain, that was the task of George Mallory.

Mallory was a 35-year-old schoolteacher and one of Britain's best climbers. Far from home, he missed his wife and three children terribly; but now, caught up in the excitement of this great adventure and seeing Everest for the first time, he wrote home to his wife, Ruth: "My job begins to show, like a flower bud soon to open out."

The mountain still lay about 140 kilometres to the west but, staring through telescopes, Mallory and his companions were beginning to get an idea of its shape. They continued westward. Finally they reached Shegar Dzong, a great hill-fortress, where they showed their special passport to the "Dzongpen", the local government official. From there they continued to Rongbuk, the monastery at the foot of Everest.

Now the men could start the detailed exploration. To some mountaineers this unlocking of a mountain's secrets is like solving a puzzle, and they find it even more exciting than attempting the summit. During that summer of 1921 it took Mallory and the others several weeks to piece together this particular jigsaw.

The team discovered that Everest is a three-sided pyramid. The south side lay in Nepal, which was still forbidden territory. Above

19

2

Rongbuk, the North Face rose up in a great triangle. There was a ridge – the North Ridge – running up the left side of this triangle, which seemed to be the best way to climb the mountain. But Everest, like most mountains, was complicated; it took several weeks before the team worked out how to get onto this ridge.

They explored everything thoroughly, including the east side of the mountain, which is also in Tibet. Here they passed through several villages, meeting the local Tibetan people. Today they still live much as they did in 1921. They are mostly farmers, harvesting potatoes and barley from small terraced fields cut into the hillside. They drink tea from China but in Tibetan fashion, with gobs of melted butter floating on top. And as there is no electricity, butter is also burned in lamps to light their homes.

The milk for the butter comes from yaks – tough, hairy, cow-like creatures that can only live at high altitude. As well as providing milk, they also carry luggage over mountain passes and pull the wooden ploughs for tilling the fields. Their dung provides manure and is used to plaster the walls of houses and, because there is so little wood in Tibet, it is also dried and burned on fires. The yaks' wool is spun and woven to produce clothing, tents and rope. Yaks are are so precious, they are rarely killed for meat.

When the British explorers arrived in 1921 it was the local people who guided them over a high pass into another valley where yaks were grazing in meadows full of flowers. This is the Kama valley, one of the most beautiful places on earth, sacred to Tibetan Buddhists.

It was now July. Everest was smothered by the monsoon – the wet

The 1921 Reconnaissance team. Back row from left: Guy Bullock, Henry Morshead, Oliver Wheeler, George Mallory. Front row from left: Alexander Heron, Alexander Wollaston, Charles Howard-Bury, Harold Raeburn.

season which brings rain (and snow a higher altitudes) to Asia. Mallory had to wait several days before a clearing in the clouds gave him a glimpse of Everest's East Face. And then it looked far too difficult and dangerous.

Nowadays it is hard to imagine wha it was like for Mallory and the team. As there was no map of Everest, the only way to find a route was to trudge on foot backwards and forwards, up and down over passes and across rivers and glaciers

At last they reached yet anothe mountain pass. Just beyond it, across a smooth snowfield, lay a climbable slope rising to a pass, or "saddle", at the start o the North Ridge. They called it the North Col, the French word for pass – a term familiar from the European Alps. Wasting no time, Mallory led a team up the 300-metre slope to reach this North Col, 7,000 metres above sea-level. At last they had a foothold on the mountain.

Even after months of hard travelling, Mallory was keen to attemp the summit before heading home. After all, the summit was only 1,800 metres higher than the North Col. But after climbing a short way Mallory realized that there was no "only" about it. He was gasping in the thin air, getting almost nowhere. The wind was bitterly cold and soon it would be winter. Those 1,800 metres were going to take all the energy of a fresh team, properly equipped for a huge climb. That would

Right: Geoffrey Bruce and George Finch returning to the North Col after their attempt at the summit

Below: a team of porters beneath the great ice wall of the North Col

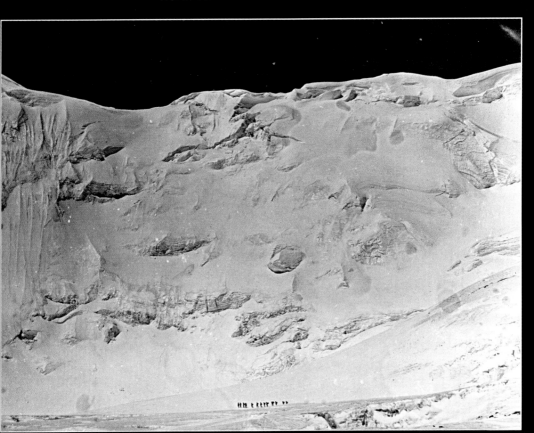

DEATH ON THE SLOPES

"Everest had claimed its first victims."

In May 1922 MALLORY was back at Rongbuk. The

leader this year was General Charles Bruce, a huge, cheerful character with a booming voice. Several tonnes of equipment and supplies had been transported 8,000 kilometres from Britain, including luxury tinned foods and several cases of champagne.

The 1922 climbers also used a team of Sherpas to help them. The Sherpas came originally from Tibet but had settled just to the south of Everest, in Nepal, about four centuries earlier. In the 1920s many of them had gone to Darjeeling to look for work. They were very tough,

Part of the 1922 team at Base Camp. From left to right: Arthur Wakefield, John Morris, Charles Bruce, Karma Paul, Edward Norton, unknown, and Geoffrey Bruce.

used to living at altitude, and seemed to be natural mountaineers. Realizing this the British team, and the foreign expeditions that came after them, employed Sherpas whenever possible to help carry the heavy loads up the mountains.

The 1922 expedition's plan was to get four climbers camping high enough up the mountain to have a chance of getting to the summit and back in a day. No one was sure how high this camp would have to be, but the conditions on the mountain meant there was a limit to how far you could travel in a single day, and the climbers were weighed down by the heavy equipment of the time. This meant they would need several other camps on the way up. Base Camp – the expedition headquarters near Rongbuk – was about 30 kilometres from the summit, and more than 3,000 metres below. It would take a small army of people to get enough supplies up the mountain and it was Bruce's job, as leader, to coordinate it all. On the lower part of the route local Tibetans as well as Sherpas were paid to carry baggage. Many of the Tibetans were women – some even carried young children on top of their loads.

After much hard work, the expedition had several tents, with food and fuel, perched on a snowy shelf at the North Col, 7,000 metres above sea-level. After sleeping here at Camp IV, the first team of Mallory, Morshead, Edward Norton and T. Howard Somervell set off, planning to pitch their tents at 8,200 metres as a base for a summit attempt the next day. Following them, five Sherpas carried the heavy equipment for this camp. To guard against the cold wind the climbers wore several layers of woollen clothing, tweed jackets and trousers, with windproof cotton jackets over the top. Their leather boots were oversized to fit extra pairs of socks inside.

Mallory led most of the way, swinging his heavy, wooden-shafted ice axe to cut footsteps in the hard snow. Nowadays, with sharp crampons on your feet, you wouldn't need to cut steps, but in 1922 they only had little nails fitted to the soles of their boots for grip. The four men were linked by a climbing rope, five metres apart. The idea was that if one man slipped, the others would hold him. That kind of "moving together" on the rope requires great skill and is only possible where the slope is not too steep. On very steep sections, the climbers usually move one at a time, with the leader anchoring himself firmly to the mountain before bringing up the others.

The day after setting off, one man did fall, pulling over two of the others. With amazing skill and speed, Mallory plunged his ice axe into the snow and wrapped the rope around it, bringing his three companions to a halt before they all took a potentially fatal fall.

The snow ridge turned to rock, with just a thin covering of fresh new snow – nothing particularly difficult, but still awkward. However, the men soon discovered their plan was impossible. They were gasping for breath, every step requiring a gigantic effort. At about 7,600 metres they just ground to a halt. The porters dumped their loads and returned to the North Col, leaving the four Englishmen to settle into Camp V.

Camping at that height was not much fun. First the climbers had to scrape away rocks to make ledges for two tents, which they would share. Once inside, the men had to make themselves as comfortable as they could, huddled inside sleeping-bags. They also needed to cook: and more importantly, drink. That meant scraping snow and ice into a pan and melting it over a primitive stove, which in those days used blocks of slow-burning solid fuel that burnt with a pathetic flame.

Morshead had got so cold that day that he was in no fit state to continue the next morning. The other three bravely carried on, but it soon became obvious that they stood no chance of getting to the summit in one day. They returned to Camp V, collected Morshead and continued down to Camp IV at the North Col.

Mallory and his companions had reached 8,225 metres – over 700 metres higher than any human had been before. Until that time no one knew whether it was possible to survive that high. They still didn't know whether a human being could drag his body another 600 metres higher, to the summit of Everest.

In 1922 aeroplane pilots were using bottled oxygen to fly to similar heights – without it they would have fainted and died. Many people thought that to get right to the summit of Everest you would need to breathe bottled oxygen. George Finch, a member of the 1922 expedition, was one of them. A few days after Mallory's attempt, Finch had a go at the summit with Geoffrey Bruce – this time breathing bottled oxygen. As Finch suspected, oxygen helped them to sleep better at night; it also enabled them climb faster than the other team had done. Finch and Bruce got even higher than Mallory's party, but Bruce had very little experience, and rather than risk getting caught by darkness near the summit Finch decided they should turn back.

There was one final attempt in 1922 but it ended in disaster almost before it had begun. The monsoon had arrived and deep new snow lay on the slope below the North Col. The Englishmen were worried, but of snow broke away, gathered speed and size, and snowballed into a team of Sherpas. The Sherpas were plucked from the slope and swept down into a crevasse. By the time Mallory and Somervell reached the Sherpas, seven men lay dead under tonnes of smothering snow. Everest had claimed its first victims. The Sherpas' bosses were filled with sorrow and guilt as they erected a memorial cairn at Base Camp with the seven men's names carved into a rock. Somervell wrote in his diary, "Why, oh why could not one of us Britishers have shared their fate?"

In 1924 the Dalai Lama gave permission for another British attempt on Chomolungma. Each expedition learns from the one before: now the climbers knew the top camp needed to be even closer to the summit. Three Sherpas, Norbu Yishang, Lhakpa Chedi and Semchumbi, carried the heavy canvas tent, sleeping bags, food and cooker to an incredible 8,168 metres above sea-level. There they left Norton and Somervell to spend the night at Camp VI. The two men did not sleep much. As for eating, this is what Norton had to say about it:

Mallory and Norton on their way to their highest point of 8,225 metres

"I know nothing which calls for more determination than this hateful duty of high altitude cooking. The process has to be repeated two or three times as, in addition to the preparation of the evening meal, o thermos flask or two must be filled with water for tomorrow's breakfast and the cooking pots must be washed up. Perhaps the most hateful part of the process is that some of the resultant mess must be eaten: there is but little desire to eat – sometimes indeed a sense of nausea at the bare idea, though of drink one cannot have enough."

The two men were away at dawn, but later that morning Somervell, croaking huskily through his dry throat, said he could go no further. So Norton continued alone over the sloping rocks. Norton was now higher than anyone had been in 1922. He had nearly reached the crest of the North-east Ridge, but he did not like the look of the great cliff on the skyline called the Second Step. Instead he stayed below the ridge, following ledges across the face of the mountain. Here nearly all the snow had been blown away by the previous winter's winds. Thinking that there was not much glare from the bare rocks, Norton removed his sun goggles to see better.

Eventually he reached a deep, snow-filled gully called the Great Couloir. Norton was climbing without bottled oxygen, yet he still managed to continue. At 8,500 metres above sea-level every step required a desperate effort. Despite the limited oxygen reaching his brain, he was thinking clearly. He knew that he could probably reach the summit, but the hardest part would be getting back down. The slightest mistake would send him tumbling nearly 3,000 metres down the North Face. Even if he did not slip, he would probably get stuck in the dark; and in the clothing he had, he would probably not survive a night in the open. Rather than risk his life, Norton decided to turn back. He reached

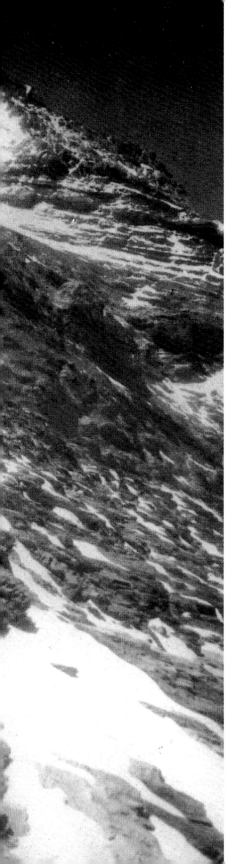

8,573 metres: a record for oxygenless climbing that would remain unbeaten for 54 years.

Climbing back towards Somervell, Norton realized just how exhausted he was. He also discovered that he had underestimated the brightness of the light at extreme altitude. After the short spell of climbing without goggles, his eyes were painful and his vision was fading. He was going snow-blind. Desperate to descend, both men got all the way down to Camp IV by nightfall. As they collapsed, exhausted, into a tent, Norton's vision finally went completely. Snow-blindness is only temporary, lasting only a day or two and causing no permanent damage, but during that couple of days it feels as if someone is rubbing grit on your eyeballs.

It was now Mallory's turn. For three years this mountain had dominated his life. He was famous throughout Britain and America as the man of Everest and he desperately wanted the summit. But at 38, he was fed up with spending so much time away from his wife and children. This was his third expedition to Tibet and he did not want to return a fourth time. He wanted to finish the job once and for all.

Mallory decided that oxygen equipment would give him the best chance of getting to the summit. Perhaps that is why instead of choosing the experienced Noel Odell to partner him he went for the youngest member of the team, 22-year-old Sandy Irvine. Irvine had little mountaineering experience but was a genius at getting the temperamental oxygen equipment to work.

Somervell took this picture of Norton as he continued for the summit alone

3

On 6 June 1924, Mallory and Irvine set off on their great quest with a small team of Sherpas who would carry additional supplies all the way up to Camp VI. Two days later, Odell climbed to Camp V where he met the Sherpas returning from Camp VI, which was where Mallory and Irvine were now set ready for their summit attempt. The Sherpas handed Odell a pencilled note from Mallory saying that the oxygen had been working well, but that it was "a bloody load for climbing". The Sherpas had another note to take down to cameraman John Noel, who hoped to film them from below:

Dear Noel,
We'll probably start early tomorrow (8th) in order to have
clear weather. It won't be too early to start looking for us
either crossing the rock band or going up the skyline at 8.00.
Yours ever,
G. Mallory

That was George Mallory's last message. No one saw him and Irvine at eight the next morning, but Odell did see them at 12.50 p.m. as he climbed up towards Camp VI. This is how he later described it:

"There was a sudden clearing of the atmosphere above me and I saw the whole summit ridge and final peak of Everest unveiled. I noticed far away on a snow slope leading up to what seemed to me to be the last step but one from the base of the final pyramid, a tiny object moving and approaching the rock step. A second object followed, and the first climbed to the top of the step. As I stood intently watching this dramatic appearance, the scene became enveloped in cloud once more, and I could not actually be certain that I saw the second figure join the first. It was of course none other than Mallory and Irvine."

Odell continued up to Camp VI. That afternoon a storm swept across the mountain. When it cleared Odell could see no sign of the two men, but he still hoped they might return later. Knowing there was not room for three in the tent, he descended to Camp IV at the North Col. Nothing was seen the next day, so on 10 June Odell climbed all the way back up to Camp VI. The tent was exactly as he had left it two days earlier. Mallory and Irvine had never returned.

Odell tied up the tent door and descended for the last time to the North Col. The others were waiting anxiously below at Camp III. From there they could see Odell arrange sleeping-bags on the white snow into a prearranged code signal. The sleeping-bags formed a dark cross. The signal meant "Death".

The mystery of Mallory's and Irvine's deaths has haunted people ever since. We still know very little about what happened on that fateful day in 1924, but there are a few clues. Nine years later Irvine's ice axe was found on some rocks near the crest of the North-east Ridge. Much later, in 1992, one of his or Mallory's empty oxygen bottles was found a little higher. Finally, in 1999, an American expedition found George Mallory's body at about 8,160 metres. It was almost perfectly preserved in the dry air where it had lain frozen for 75 years.

His skull was damaged, one elbow dislocated and both bones of his right leg broken. His chest was bruised by a vicious tug from a hemp

The last known photograph of Mallory and Irvine, taken on 6 June by Odell

climbing rope, still tangled around his body. One end of the rope was tied around his waist; the other had snapped.

Mallory had been killed in a terrible fall and the rope joining the two men had broken, possibly sliced by a sharp rock. Perhaps Irvine or Mallory slipped, pulling the other off. The two men were probably climbing back down through the Yellow Band when the accident happened. They may even have been returning from the summit.

My own feeling is that, like Norton, Mallory and Irvine were probably forced to turn back before getting to the top. Perhaps one day we shall know more. If someone finds the camera Mallory and Irvine are believed to have been carrying, perhaps there will be photos inside of the summit. But nothing will take away the sadness and pain suffered by each of their families. As Mallory's wife wrote to a friend: "Whether he got to the top of the mountain or did not, whether he lived or died, makes no difference to my admiration for him... If only it hadn't happened! It so easily might not have."

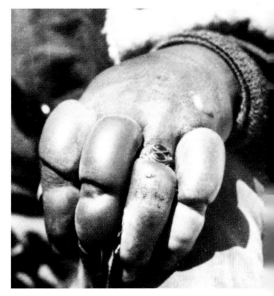

Sherpa Namgya's swollen, frostbitten hands

Mallory and Irvine were not the only men to die in 1924. A month earlier, before the expedition even reached the North Col, a Nepalese Gurkha soldier called Shamsher died of a stroke. He was buried near Base Camp. And another man, Manbahadur, the expedition cobbler, got terrible frostbite.

Frostbite happens when warm blood stops reaching the parts of the body furthest from the heart, usually fingers and toes. The skin goes white and loses all feeling. If it is serious frostbite, it then turns purple and eventually black. Often large blisters swell up like balloons. If the frostbite has not struck too deep, fingers and toes usually recover after a few weeks. The dead black layer peels off and new fresh skin appears underneath. But with really serious frostbite, the flesh is frozen right through to the bone, it dies and eventually rots away. Many people have lost toes, fingers, or even whole hands and feet on Everest. In 1924 Manbahadur's feet were frostbitten right up to the ankles. He was carried down to Base Camp, but then his feet got gangrene – an infection which can poison the whole body.

In 1924 the only cure was to amputate the rotten limb, but Everest Base Camp was not equipped for amputations. Poor Manbahadur became terribly ill as infection spread through his body, and he too died. Before leaving Rongbuk in 1924, the climbers had to add four new names to the stone memorial at Base Camp. It was a sad team that set off on the long march home.

There were no more Everest attempts for nine years. Then no fewer than four British expeditions attempted the mountain, in 1933, 1935, 1936 and 1938. None of them managed to reach the summit. In 1933 a climber called Frank Smythe reached Norton's high point. Like Norton, Smythe was climbing alone. At one point he stopped to eat some chocolate. He broke off a piece and turned to hand it to his companion. Then realized that there was no companion. At extreme altitude, many climbers have felt or seen an imaginary person beside them – probably the result of not having enough oxygen in the brain.

You may wonder why climbers like Smythe didn't use bottled oxygen to help them. There were several reasons. Whatever Finch had said in 1922, the equipment was still unreliable, and it was extremely heavy. If you were going to carry 13.5 kilograms extra weight on your back, you wanted to be sure it was going to help you.

Bill Tilman, leader of the 1938 expedition, believed that climbing with bottled oxygen would be like cheating. He also felt expeditions had become far too big and expensive. His friend Eric Shipton, who had been on all of the 1930s expeditions, agreed. He and Tilman had climbed many peaks over 7,000 metres in the Himalaya – often just the two of them and a couple of Sherpas to share the adventure.

During the 1930s Shipton spent every summer in the Himalaya. In September 1939 he was camped on a remote glacier called Snow Lake, in the far north of India, when news came through that Britain was at war with Germany. The Second World War had begun and all dreams of Everest would have to be forgotten for a very long time.

*Expedition porters carry
huge loads into the Western Cwm*

FINDING A ROUTE

"Sometimes it is wise to listen to the advice of your elders. At other times it is better to ignore it…"

Tenzing IS A COMMON Sherpa name, but there was

only one Tenzing Norgay. Norgay means "fortunate one", and despite his humble background Tenzing Norgay seems to have been destined for great things. Strictly speaking he was not a Sherpa, because he was born in Tibet rather than Nepal, in a tiny village on the east side of Everest. He was a young boy when the tweed-jacketed British explorers walked through the village in 1921, looking for Everest.

Later his family moved to Nepal, to live in the Sherpa village of Thame, on the south side of the mountain. As a young man, Tenzing Norgay then travelled to Darjeeling to look for work, and it was there that he signed on for Eric Shipton's 1935 Everest expedition.

Mountaineering was a job of work for the Sherpas, but for Tenzing it became more than that. He started to love climbing for its own sake and began to dream that he himself might one day reach the summit of Chomolungma.

After the Second World War, Tenzing became friendly with some of the famous Swiss mountaineers of the day, joining them on some of the great unclimbed summits of the Indian Himalaya. Then in 1947 Tenzing returned to the north side of Everest with a Canadian called Earl Denman who wanted to try the mountain illegally. Together they got as far as Camp III but no further. At least he returned safely.

Then in 1950 the Chinese Communist army invaded Tibet. Suddenly this huge country became part of China. Chinese troops gathered along the Himalayan frontier, making it quite clear that foreigners were not welcome. There was now no hope of any foreign expedition visiting the north side of Everest.

Luckily for mountaineers, just as one door closed, another opened. In 1947 the King of Nepal allowed Bill Tilman to visit the unknown, unmapped mountain interior of his country. Tilman explored the mountains around the Langtang valley, and in the autumn of 1950 he joined some American friends who had permisson to look at the south side of Everest itself.

Tilman only saw the lower part of Everest's Nepal side and he was quite gloomy about what he saw, but a new generation of mountaineers were keen to take up the Everest challenge. One of them, a young

British surgeon called Michael Ward, was spending all his spare time in London at the Royal Geographical Society, studying maps and photos. He found some aerial photographs taken from about 9,000 metres by a Spitfire pilot in 1945. One of the photos showed the top part of Everest's South-east Ridge. No one had ever seen this ridge properly, but from this photo it appeared climbable. And it lay in Nepal. Perhaps Everest could be climbed this way.

Sometimes it is wise to listen to the advice of your elders. At other times it is better to ignore it. Ward decided to ignore Tilman's gloomy advice and go to have a proper look at the southern side of Everest for himself. So the 1951 Everest Reconnaissance was born. Its job was to see if there was a practical route up Everest from the south.

The Spitfire pilot's shot of Everest

Ward's friend Bill Murray did all the hard work of organizing supplies and equipment and a young rocket scientist called Tom Bourdillon joined the team. At the last minute the young men invited the grand old man of Everest, Eric Shipton, to be their leader.

Shipton, like Tilman, did not rate the chances of a southern route very highly. But this opportunity to visit the Nepalese homeland of the Sherpa people was too good to turn down. He would have a wonderful time, visiting old friends, meeting their families and sharing their home-made barley beer, called "chang". He would also have a chance to explore a region of unknown mountains.

While Shipton was preparing for Nepal, a team of young New Zealanders was experiencing its own first Himalayan expedition, in India. They wondered whether they might come on to Nepal and join the British expedition? Shipton knew how tough New Zealand climbers could be. Their Southern Alps were famous for difficult ice climbing and

37

The 1951 team. Standing from left: Shipton, Murray, Bourdillon, Riddiford. Sitting from left: Ward and Hillary.

long, hard approaches through dense forest – perfect training for the Himalaya. Shipton wrote back to say, "Yes, two of you can join us, but you must bring your own food." One of the chosen two was a 30-year-old bee-keeper from Auckland called Edmund Hillary. And so, in a dream come true, Hillary found himself in Nepal, climbing with his great hero Eric Shipton, exploring a completely new route up the highest mountain on earth.

The job of the 1951 Reconnaissance was to see whether it was possible to enter the Western Cwm. Cwm (pronounced "coom") is a Welsh word meaning a bowl-shaped valley. Mallory had used the name to describe the secret valley on Everest's south side. All Mallory could see from Tibet was a great jumble of ice-blocks, tumbling out of the hidden valley – what mountaineers call an ice fall. Mallory named it the Khumbu Icefall. Any climbers wanting to reach the Western Cwm would have to get up this ice fall first, and it looked extremely nasty.

Climbers working their way through the Khumbu Icefall

It was the Khumbu Icefall that Tilman had been so gloomy about in 1950. Now, in 1951, Shipton's team climbed high up a slope near by to get a better look. To them the Icefall didn't look quite so bad. Also, they could see beyond it — right into the secret valley of the Western Cwm. The valley looked reasonable and the snow wall beyond it looked possible. Above that lay a huge saddle called the South Col, and above that was the South-east Ridge which the Spitfire pilot had photographed. Perhaps Everest really was possible this way!

First they had to check the Icefall. It took the six men several days to climb it. Hillary turned out to be a fine ice craftsman, swinging his ice axe with great skill.

The Icefall was certainly dangerous. The whole mass of jumbled blocks was slowly tipping down the valley. It was not a place to hang around. But the men managed to pick their way through the labyrinth until only one huge, gaping crevasse separated them from the smooth snow floor of the Western Cwm. The crevasse could be bridged with a ladder but this expedition was not equipped for a full-scale attempt on the

4

After the great 1951 success in the Khumbu Icefall, Eric Shipton found some mysterious footprints on a glacier west of Everest. He published these photographs saying they might show the print of the yeti, or "abominable snowman". Some people think he might have made the close-up prints himself; others believe they are genuine. No one is quite sure if the yeti does exist, but there are bears in the Himalaya that do sometimes stand on two legs.

mountain. The Reconnaissance had achieved its target for this year and Michael Ward's idea had been proved correct – this was a possible route to the summit. Next year they would return to complete the job.

Back in London, Ward was furious to discover that the Everest Committee had not managed to get a permit for 1952. Only one permit was given each year and the Nepalese government had decided that in 1952 Everest would be reserved for a Swiss expedition led by René Dittert. For the first time a nation other than Britain was to have a chance at mountaineering's greatest prize!

In 1952, few British climbers had the skill and experience of the finest Swiss climbers. After all, the Swiss lived right among the Alps. They had also maximized their chances by getting permission for two attempts – one before and one after the monsoon season. The monsoon storms of June to August made climbing Everest virtually impossible; most attempts are made in spring, but if the Swiss spring attempt failed they could try again in October. It looked as though they would snatch the great Everest prize from under the noses of the British. And they very nearly did. In fact, the Swiss got even higher than Edward Norton had done in 1924. Following the new southern route, they fixed ropes through the Khumbu Icefall, making it safe for teams of Sherpas to carry equipment up into the Western Cwm. They called this extraordinary, magical place "The Valley of Silence". They continued up its smooth sloping floor, then up the 1,200-metre wall above, eventually reaching the South Col.

The Swiss discovered that the South Col is a huge open expanse, as big as several football pitches. It is like a vast natural funnel for the wind, which scours away any soft snow. All that is left is ice, rubble and compressed snow. No tent can stand the wind's blast for long.

It was here that the Swiss prepared for the final climb to the summit. However, they had not brought enough equipment to the South Col, so ended up with two climbers at an even higher camp on the South-east Ridge with no stove to melt snow (so they had nothing to drink) and no sleeping-bags. Despite their terrible, sleepless, thirsty night, the two climbers managed to continue the next day. But there was a problem with their oxygen sets, which only seemed to work when they were not moving, so they had to stop every two or three steps to suck on their oxygen masks. Then they would continue, struggling under the weight of the heavy oxygen sets as a vicious wind blasted snow against their goggles. Frozen, exhausted and bitterly disappointed, they had to admit it was hopeless and turn back. But they had reached a record height of 8,600 metres,

One of the two men who so nearly made it to the summit in 1952 was a mountain guide from Geneva called Raymond Lambert. The other was Tenzing Norgay. His boyhood dream had almost come true. He returned after the monsoon, for the second Swiss attempt. But by October the winter winds were starting to batter the mountain, making movement virtually impossible. The climbers could go no further than the South Col. The Swiss had failed to reach the summit.

Tenzing returned to his wife and two daughters in Darjeeling. He was exhausted but determined to recover quickly over the winter. In March 1953 another British expedition would be arriving in Nepal and he wanted to be part of it. If the gods would allow it, this time he would be going all the way to the top.

Above: the oxygen-cylinder gong at Thyangboche Monastery – rung at 5.00 p.m. to instruct women to leave the monastery

Above: the 1953 team

Right: the vast snowfield of the Western Cwm

THE FINAL RIDGE

"Bourdillon and Evans had an agonizing
decision to make. Although the oxygen
equipment had worked very well, the
cylinders would not last for ever."

5

While THE SWISS WERE at

work on Everest in 1952, Eric Shipton was leading a British training expedition to some mountains about 60 kilometres to the west. They had Everest booked for 1953 and just hoped that the Swiss would not reach the top first. For the expedition scientist, Dr Griffith Pugh, it was a chance to test new equipment, food rations, tents and clothing. Most important of all, he wanted to test the oxygen equipment. He was convinced that the only way to get to the summit of Everest was by using bottled oxygen. And he wanted it to work perfectly.

John Hunt at the South Col

Shipton was not so sure. All his old doubts about big expeditions came back. Did he really want to lead an invasion of Everest? Did he really want to lug all that heavy equipment to the South Col? Back in London, the Everest Committee began to worry about Shipton's doubts. Perhaps he was not the right man to lead the 1953 expedition after all? It was now autumn 1952 and it looked as though the Swiss were not going to succeed. But they had permission to return in 1955 and the French had Everest booked for 1954. If Britain really wanted the first ascent, 1953 was probably the last chance.

In fact, no one could guarantee success. Mountaineering is not like that, particularly on Everest. Nevertheless, the committee felt that Shipton was not determined enough. At the last minute they decided to appoint a new leader. The 1953 expedition would be led by an army officer called Brigadier John Hunt.

It was a wonderful opportunity for Hunt, but also embarrassing. He had always admired Shipton and knew how much this would hurt him. But Shipton was very honourable and advised all the team to work hard for the new leader. So John Hunt set up an office at the Royal Geographical Society to start preparing for the great adventure. This time, nothing would be left to chance.

Hunt knew that equipment was vital. He also knew that the most important thing of all was to have a good team who would work well together. Many of the climbers had already been chosen. Charles Wylie, another army officer, was in charge of organizing all the equipment and transport. Tom Bourdillon was working on oxygen equipment with Dr Griffith Pugh and the other doctor, Michael Ward. Alf Gregory was in charge of photography. Tom Stobart would make the film. The deputy leader was a very experienced mountaineer called Charles Evans.

At first they were all quite prickly towards the new leader and at one point it looked as though some of them would resign. But Hunt clearly meant business. He worked extremely hard and was efficient. And more importantly, he was warm-hearted and friendly. He had a gift for making people feel valued. And he was determined that the whole team would be sharing this great adventure.

The other British climbers insisted that Hunt should also include the two New Zealanders – George Lowe and Edmund Hillary. Both men were good mountaineers and capable of reaching the summit. Hunt agreed.

On an Everest expedition people often get ill, so it helps to have fresh climbers, ready to take over when others have to rest. Hunt certainly felt that an enlarged team would increase the chances of success. First he asked Wilfred Noyce to join them. Like Mallory before him, Noyce was a schoolmaster, a very fine climber and a talented writer. He was now in his thirties, the age when most climbers are strongest at altitude. Hunt also wanted to include two younger climbers. Various candidates came for interview, and in the end he chose Michael Westmacott and George Band, both in their early twenties. James Morris, a journalist from "The Times", who were again sponsoring the expedition, would also join the team.

Everyone worked extremely hard over the winter. Hunt wrote a detailed plan showing how much equipment had to be carried to each camp. Pugh, Ward and Bourdillon worked furiously to get the oxygen equipment ready. Famous companies such as Kodak and Rolex provided equipment. Special new high-altitude boots were made and aluminium ladders were ordered for the Icefall. Everything, including clothing and equipment for the Sherpas, had to be packed in wooden crates, then shipped to India. Just before leaving London, Hunt was summoned to Buckingham Palace. Queen Elizabeth II had just succeeded to the throne the previous year, though she was yet to be crowned. Her husband, Prince Philip, was patron to the expedition and wanted to hear about all the plans for Everest.

In March the whole team gathered at Kathmandu, the capital of Nepal. Some of the team had flown direct to the new airport, but most of them had come by ship to India, then by rail, and finally on foot. In 1953 there was still no road to Kathmandu, which sits in a valley surrounded by mountains. All goods from India, including the Everest expedition baggage, arrived on a special rope cableway.

One of the last to arrive in Kathmandu was Edmund Hillary. It was late summer in New Zealand, and right up to the last minute he had been helping his father with the bees. Now he had finally got away.

In Kathmandu they were also joined by Tenzing Norgay. He would be the "sirdar" – the headman in charge of all the Sherpas. This was probably the most important job on the whole expedition; but as well as being sirdar, Tenzing would be a member of the climbing team. His summit dream might finally come true.

Today, most expeditions to the southern side of Everest fly from Kathmandu, landing just a few miles from the mountain at a tiny airstrip. In 1953 the only way to get there was on foot, all the way from Kathmandu. In many ways this long approach, taking nearly three weeks, was a great advantage for the team. It was a chance to get fit and an opportunity to gradually adapt their bodies to altitude – a process called acclimatization. Best of all, it was a chance to see some of the most beautiful country on earth.

Unlike the old pre-war approach from Tibet, this trek was through a soft, green land. For the first few days, walking alongside paddy fields, it was very hot. Later, the climbers crossed cooler high ridges, passing through forests of rhododendrons.

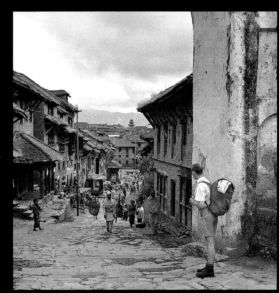

Wilfred Noyce on the cobbled streets of the village of Bhadgaon

Thyangboche Monastery with the expedition camp in the foreground

Every few kilometres the team would pass through another village. Most of these had beautifully paved streets, even though no wheeled vehicle had ever passed this way. Everything was carried on the backs of men and women, and the same was true of the Everest expedition. When the final packing of all the supplies and equipment was complete, Wylie had 350 loads, each weighing around 27 kilograms, to transport to Base Camp. Now the long line of 350 porters snaked its way up through the hills for 17 days. Twelve more men were employed to carry all the coins needed to pay the porters.

As the expedition got close to Everest the landscape became more and more dramatic. They were now in the valley of the Khumbu — the river that flows out of Everest's Khumbu Glacier. The whole area is called Sola Khumbu, and it is here that the Sherpas live. A long, grinding path leads steeply to the main Sherpa village, Namche Bazar.

The following day the expedition halted further up the valley at Thyangboche Monastery. Like the Tibetans, the Sherpas are Buddhist followers of the Dalai Lama. In fact their monastery was founded by the same monk who founded Rongbuk. Hanging at the entrance of Thyangboche was an unusual gong — an old oxygen cylinder, carried over from Tibet before the Second World War; a relic of the early attempts on Everest. On doctors' advice, Hunt decided that the team needed lots more time to acclimatize; rather than rush straight onto the mountain, they would spend three weeks at Thyangboche.

47

It was a lovely campsite, on a grassy meadow beside the monastery. From here Everest itself was hidden, but there were other mountains all around – some of the most spectacular peaks on earth. Hardly any of them had been climbed and many of them looked ferociously difficult. Splitting into groups, the climbers explored the country around Thyangboche, making first ascents of a number of peaks around 6,000 metres. All the time their lungs were coping better with the thin air and their bodies were producing more haemoglobin – the red blood cells which carry oxygen from the lungs to the rest of the body. The stay at the monastery also allowed time for more bottled oxygen tests. Then the time came to leave the meadows of Thyangboche. By 21 April the whole team had moved up the valley to Base Camp. The serious work had begun.

Base Camp was not a pretty spot, but it was the only suitable place close enough to the mountain. There was not a tree, not even a blade of grass, in sight. The tents were pitched on stony rubble and beneath the rubble lay ice – the ice of the Khumbu Glacier. Immediately above camp the ice reared up for 600 metres in a jumble of tottering towers: the Icefall.

By the time the main party arrived, Hillary, Lowe, Band and Westmacott had already started work on the Icefall. It had changed completely since Hillary was there two years earlier; even during the course of the 1953 expedition it would change again. Towers would shift and crumple, crevasses would open up. It would always be dangerous. The trick was just to keep those dangers to a minimum. Hillary chose a route where men could move as quickly as possible through the danger zones. Each zone had its own name, such as "Atom Bomb Area", "Mike's Horror" and "Hellfire Alley". In the hardest sections rope handrails were fixed to metal stakes driven into the ice. The biggest crevasses were spanned with aluminium ladders, but the expedition didn't have enough ladders and had to send someone down the valley to fetch tree trunks for additional bridges.

One day, coming down through the Icefall, Hillary couldn't be bothered to inch across one of the bridges, and decided to jump instead. He leaped across the crevasse, and as he landed on the far edge he felt the ice shift under his crampons. Then it crumbled. The whole edge of the crevasse began to topple backwards, with Hillary attached. He was falling backwards into the chasm. At the last minute there was jerk on the rope round his waist, the great chunk of ice

George Lowe (top) and John Hunt climbing an ice wall in the Khumbu Icefall

tumbled into the depths and Hillary was left hanging, breathless but alive. The man holding the other end of the rope was Tenzing Norgay.

Hillary and Tenzing made a great partnership. The team was still a long way from the top, but Hillary began to hope that perhaps he and Tenzing would be chosen for one of the summit teams. Not everyone

5

would get a chance. Two or three pairs – at the most – would try, and that could only happen when enough stores had reached the South Col.

You might wonder why it took so many people just to get two or three pairs close to the summit. In those days no one believed it was possible to climb all the way from Base Camp to summit in one go. It was a journey of several kilometres and nearly 3,700 metres of ascent. Equipment had improved a lot since the twenties, but it was still very heavy, especially the oxygen equipment. Hunt hoped, like the Swiss, to place the top camp higher than the South Col. That would take six men and they would need oxygen. Getting that oxygen, plus tents, sleeping-bags and stoves to the South Col would take many more men. They would have to start from a large camp in the Western Cwm, which in turn would take even more men, and more supplies to build, and so on. It was a long, complicated process. In the end, including Base Camp, nine camps were placed on the mountain. All this took several weeks.

Nowadays many expeditions repeat the 1953 route. Generally most of the leading is done by highly experienced Sherpas. But in 1953 most Sherpas were not experienced at leading expeditions, and the foreigners were in charge of choosing and fixing the route. They were also responsible for the Sherpas' safety. Mike Westmacott's job, for instance, was overseeing the dangerous route through the Icefall.

A heavily-laden team avoids a huge crevasse in the Western Cwm

At the top of the Icefall, the long trail continued up the snow floor of the Western Cwm to Camp IV. This camp became the real base for the expedition.

route lay up a great wall of snow and ice on the side of Lhotse, a mountain to the south of Everest and the fourth highest peak in the world. They had climbed about a thousand metres up this wall, the Lhotse Face, before moving diagonally left onto the great shelf of the South Col. Now it was the turn of the British to repeat that long journey.

This is where the 1953 expedition got into serious difficulties. Several of the climbers were getting ill. Either they had picked up stomach bugs, or the thin dry air was giving them coughs and sore throats. Even some of the Sherpas were finding it tough. Slogging up the Lhotse Face with their heavy loads they began to run out of steam. Charles Wylie and Wilfred Noyce worked incredibly hard to keep things moving, but they could not go on for ever.

Then Hillary and Tenzing went up to help. Hillary was very fit and determined and Tenzing was also going well. Tenzing had the advantage of being the Shepa sirdar, too, admired and trusted by other Sherpas. He gave them confidence and they began to work harder.

At last, on 21 May, Noyce and Sherpa Anullu reached the South Col, where they found the remains of the 1952 Swiss camp. Only a few tattered shreds of cotton remained attached to the metal poles; the rest had been swept by the wind into Tibet.

The next day fourteen Sherpas climbed up the Lhotse Face, each carrying a vital load. Leading were Wylie, Hillary and Tenzing. One of the Sherpas felt unwell, so the three climbers took his load to the South Col

Everest from near Base Camp on the Khumbu Glacier

Over the next three days more loads were carried up and the lead climbers arrived on the Col to settle into Camp VIII. Now, at last, the final climb to the summit could begin.

John Hunt decided that there would be two summit attempts. The first pair of climbers would try from Camp VIII on the South Col. Even if they did not reach the summit, he hoped that they would get very close. Their attempt would be a kind of reconnaissance. The second team would start from an even higher Camp IX, with a better chance of reaching the top. If they failed, he would have to think about a third attempt. But it was now the last week of May and the bad monsoon weather would soon be coming. Time was running out. Over the next few days things were going to be very tense at the South Col.

Tom Bourdillon and Charles Evans were chosen for the first attempt. They would use a special oxygen system where you breathe almost pure oxygen. No one was quite sure how well this "closed-circuit" system would work, but in theory it ought to help them climb much faster.

They left the South Col on the morning of 26 May. Following behind more slowly were John Hunt and Sherpa Da Namgyal, who were going to climb part of the way up the South-east Ridge to leave supplies ready for the second summit party's top camp. They followed the tracks of Bourdillon and Evans up a steep snow gully and onto the crest of the ridge. Already Hunt was feeling very tired – he didn't know at the time that ice had been blocking the tube from his oxygen cylinder; and Da Namgyal was even more tired. At about 8,400 metres they had to stop and dump the supplies then returned to Camp VIII. There they waited anxiously for news of Bourdillon and Evans.

With their special oxygen system, the two men were moving very fast. Well, fast by Everest standards. Four hours after leaving the South Col they had climbed over 600 metres. They passed the point reached by Lambert and Tenzing the previous year and continued, higher than anyone had been before. The ridge steepened. Flaky loose snow threatened to break away, sending them tumbling 3,000 metres down the East Face. So Evans kicked his way left onto some yellowish rocks, part of the same Yellow Band the pre-war climbers had found on the North Face. The only sound was the hiss of oxygen through his mask and the scratching of crampons on the rock. He knew from the Spitfire photographs that he was getting close to the South Summit – a bump on the ridge just a short way from the summit of Everest itself.

At one o'clock that afternoon a group of Sherpas arrived at the South Col with supplies. Staring up, they saw two tiny dots crawling onto a pointed white summit. They began to shout excitedly, rejoicing. But in fact the true summit was hidden. A thousand metres above them, the two tiny dots, Bourdillon and Evans, were standing on the South Summit. The final ridge was still ahead of them.

No human being had ever seen this final ridge. It was a narrow crest of rock, topped with great blobs of snow, called cornices, which stuck out precariously to the right, over the immense drop of the East Face. On the left, the rocks sloped away steeply towards the 2,400-metre precipice of the South-west Face.

At the far end of the knife-edge was a sudden step – a cliff nearly eighteen metres high – the height of a large house. Above that things looked easier, but there were still dangerous cornices bulging out to the right. The actual summit was still out of sight.

Bourdillon and Evans had an agonizing decision to make. Although the oxygen equipment had worked very well, the cylinders would not last for ever. This final ridge looked hard. It might take five hours to get to the summit and back. By then the oxygen would have run out and it would be nearly dark. And they would still have to descend around 900 metres to the South Col.

Taking off his mask to speak, gasping at the sudden lack of oxygen, Evans told Bourdillon they ought to turn back now. Bourdillon suggested they just go a little bit further. While Evans paid out the rope, the younger man edged his way a little further. But he soon stopped. It was too risky. Everest was not worth dying for. Bitterly disappointed, he made the brave decision to turn round.

As they were heading down, the two men left a spare half-full cylinder of oxygen near the South Summit, ready for the second team to use. As many future climbers would learn, it is a long way down from the there. Bourdillon and Evans were very tired – by the time they got back to the South Col they were utterly finished.

Right: Hillary and Tenzing climbing the gully to the South-east Ridge

Edmund Hillary (top) and Tenzing Norgay

SUCCESS AT LAST

"Hillary held out his mittened hand for Tenzing to shake. But Tenzing flung his arms around Hillary, thumping his back joyfully."

Bourdillon AND EVANS had done a fantastic

job. Now Hunt knew what the second team could expect to find on the final stretch to the summit. He had chosen the men for the second team some time ago and now they had arrived at the South Col: Edmund Hillary and Tenzing Norgay.

That night of 26 May the tents shook and rattled in the wind. No one got much sleep. In the morning it was too windy for Hillary and Tenzing to set off towards the summit. Instead, Hillary helped Bourdillon and Evans prepare to descend to the Western Cwm, and at midday they set off with one of the Sherpas. Bourdillon was stumbling like a drunk man and clearly needed help.

For the leader, John Hunt, this was the hardest moment of the expedition. He wanted desperately to stay at the South Col, close to the action, but he had to admit that he too was getting weak. No human can survive for long above 8,000 metres and he realized that someone else had to go down with Evans and Bourdillon. He turned to Hillary and said, "The most important thing is for you chaps to come back safely. Remember that. But get up if you can." He waved goodbye and set off back down.

That afternoon the wind died down at the South Col. Hillary spent much of the day checking equipment – in particular the oxygen equipment – and discussing plans with George Lowe, his fellow New Zealander. Lowe would be helping carry loads to the new high camp the next day.

The next day, 28 May, Edmund Hillary, Tenzing Norgay, George Lowe, Alf Gregory and Sherpa Nyima set off from the Col. The expedition film-maker was out of sight, far below in the Western Cwm, but he had given George Lowe a small cine camera. Gregory was taking still photos. Tenzing had the flags of Great Britain, Nepal, India and the United Nations wrapped ready round the shaft of his ice axe. He hoped with all his heart that tomorrow he would be holding them up on top of the world.

Soon after reaching the South-east Ridge they passed the remains of the tent where Tenzing had spent such a miserable, shivering night with Raymond Lambert the previous year. Then

they reached the supplies Hunt and Da Namgyal had left earlier.

The plan was to put the top camp even higher than this. So now, the five men had to share out the extra weight, on top of the burden they were already carrying. With the tent, stove, sleeping-bags, food and oxygen equipment it was a terrible burden. Each man was now carrying at least 22 kilograms on his back; Hillary was carrying 28.5 kilograms. Even with the help of oxygen-breathing equipment, that was an astonishing weight to be carrying above 8,200 metres.

They stopped eventually a short way below the South Summit. Lowe, Gregory and Nyima dumped their loads and wished the other

Hillary and Tenzing pause on the South-east Ridge

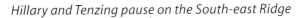

two luck, then they set off down. At about 8,500 metres, Hillary and Tenzing started chopping with their ice axes, making a ledge for the tent. The best they could manage was a sort of double ledge, like two steps of a staircase, dug into the side of the mountain. They pitched the tent on this double ledge. Then Tenzing climbed onto the lower ledge, with Hillary perched above him, leaning back against the side of the mountain, and settled down for the night.

Things had come a long way since the twenties. Both men wore padded down-filled trousers and jackets inside their down sleeping-bags. Under their sleeping-bags, air mattresses insulated them from the snow. Hillary lit the paraffin Primus stove and managed to melt snow for drinks of soup and lemonade, accompanied by biscuits, sardines, jam, honey, dates and tinned apricots. None of these foods needed cooking but provided a mixture of all the things the body needs from food, namely carbohydrate, sugar, fat and protein. While they were eating, Hillary was also doing mental arithmetic. The oxygen could be set at different levels; for climbing they needed to breathe at least two litres per minute, ideally three or four. But for resting and sleeping they could manage on one litre per minute.

During the night there were some hard gusts of wind. At one point the two men had to brace themselves against the tent to make sure they were not blown off the mountain. But then it calmed and they slept, warm inside their sleeping-bags.

At 4.00 a.m. on the morning of 29 May Hillary sat up and lit the stove to make breakfast. It was a perfect, still dawn. Tenzing pointed out to Hillary the Thyangboche Monastery, a tiny rectangle in the blue valley mist, 4,800 metres below. God is good to us, he thought. Chomolungma is good to us.

It was time to get ready. As Hillary began to pull on his climbing boots he realized that they were frozen stiff – he had forgotten to keep them warm inside his sleeping-bag, so he had to thaw them out over the stove until the leather was soft enough to pull over his feet. Tenzing, on the other hand, had kept his boots on all night. When Hillary's boots were ready, they both strapped on their crampons. Then they

Tenzing and Hillary check their oxygen equipment before leaving the Western Cwm. Hillary's striped headgear protects his face from the fierce sun. Tenzing has the flags wrapped ready around his ice axe.

59

shouldered their pack frames, each with two full oxygen cylinders. Hillary checked masks, supply tubes and valves. Then they crawled out of the tent, onto the slope outside and began, step by step, to move towards the South Summit.

At that altitude you are so high in the earth's atmosphere that the sky is a deep blue, almost black. The snow glitters brilliantly and you can see for hundreds of kilometres.

The two men followed the tracks left by Bourdillon and Evans two days earlier. As they got close to the South Summit they found the spare oxygen Evans had left. Hillary did more sums, calculating how much he and Tenzing had left to get to the summit and back. By starting from such a high camp, they had a really good chance of doing it.

At 9.00 a.m. they reached the South Summit and saw the final ridge for themselves. Evans had told Hillary he thought it might be impossible, but Hillary was determined to give it a try. He descended from the South Summit, with Tenzing following on the rope. Then he started to make his way along the knife-edge ridge, swinging his axe to cut steps. To his surprise he was enjoying himself! It was like a good day in the New Zealand Alps.

But then they reached the step in the ridge. On the left was a steep cliff of brown rock. On the right was a vertical slab of snow, hanging out over the East Face. Then Hillary noticed a crack, like a chimney, between the rock and the snow. He asked Tenzing to watch the rope carefully, then set to work.

He wedged his huge, cramponed, size-twelve right boot in the chimney while his left foot scratched on the rock, searching for small holds and ledges. Facing left, with his back pushed against the snow, he heaved and squirmed up the chimney. He just prayed that the snow would not come away and send him catapulting backwards down the East Face.

With the oxygen turned up full at four litres per minute, he wriggled his way up the cliff, foot by foot. At last he reached a rock spike at the top, made himself secure, and shouted to Tenzing to follow. Ever since that day in 1953, that final cliff on the South-east Ridge has been called the Hillary Step.

Now that he and Tenzing were above it, Hillary was fairly certain nothing could stop them. But, as they discovered, the summit was still quite a bit further.

Taking no chances, Hillary cut steps all the way. Step by step, they made their way along the snow ridge, taking great care not to tread on the big cornices which hung out over space, on the right. Several times they reached a curved mound of snow only to see another one ahead. Finally, Hillary realized he was looking over the top and could see down the far side of the mountain. A few more whacks of the ice axe and he stood with Tenzing on top of the world. It was 11.30 a.m.

Hillary held out his mittened hand for Tenzing to shake. But Tenzing flung his arms around Hillary, thumping his back joyfully. Then he unfurled the flags on his ice axe and held them high against the blue sky. Hillary removed his mittens, got out his camera and took a photo of Tenzing. Then, to prove without a doubt that they really had reached the summit, he took photos looking down the mountain in every direction.

Tenzing at the summit holding aloft his ice axe with the flags of the United Nations, Great Britain, Nepal and India

Looking down to the north, Tenzing could see the Rongbuk Glacier in Tibet. That was where he had been 18 years earlier, working on his first Everest expedition. Looking to the east, he could see the meadows, far, far beneath him, where he had helped look after the yaks as a young boy. Now, after all those years his dream had come true. He said a silent Tibetan prayer: "Tuji Chey, Chomolungma – I am grateful". Then he buried in the snow some offerings for the gods, including some sweets given to him by his daughter Nima. Hillary buried the small cross that Hunt had given him. Then they added the four flags.

The summit of Everest is a huge blob of snow many metres thick. Most of the year it is blasted by westerly winds, pushing and blowing it out to the east. Gradually the snow bulges out and curls over. So anything left on the summit eventually works its way down the East Face; by the time a Swiss team made the second ascent of Everest, in 1955, there was no sign of Hillary's and Tenzing's visit.

Hillary and Tenzing knew that the hardest part would be going down. They took great care and made it safely back to their tent by 2.00 p.m. They stopped there to make a drink, then carried on down. That evening they were at the South Col, telling their wonderful story to Noyce and Lowe. Everyone else was further down the mountain. The radio could not transmit from the South Col, so no one else in the world knew that Everest had been climbed.

It was only the next day that the others heard the great news. Waiting anxiously in the Western Cwm, Hunt watched the figures coming down the Lhotse Face. They moved slowly and wearily. As they plodded across the flat snow of the Cwm, they looked miserable. Hunt's heart sank. Then the first figure, George Lowe, held up a thumb. He raised his ice axe and pointed back up at the summit. Suddenly everyone started to run towards the descending figures. Hunt rushed up to Hillary and Tenzing, threw his arms round them and congratulated them on their wonderful success.

Everest had been climbed, but no one outside the Western Cwm knew. James Morris, the journalist on the expedition, now had to send his report back to London. It was now 30 May. He suddenly remembered that on 2 June, Queen Elizabeth II was going to be crowned. Wouldn't it be wonderful if he could get the news back to London for Coronation Day!

Over mugs of tea, Hillary and Tenzing told James Morris their story.

After their gruelling climb to the summit, Tenzing and Hillary enjoy
a well-earned rest and a cup of tea at Camp IV

Then he set off down. Morris was not a mountaineer, but somehow, with help from Westmacott, he managed to hurry down the dangerous Icefall, reaching Base Camp after dark.

He got out his typewriter and wrote his report and prepared a telegram to go first. It was written in code, to stop any rival reporters stealing his news. He typed: "Snow conditions bad stop advanced base abandoned yesterday stop awaiting improvement". Only at "The Times" office would they know that this actually meant: "Summit of Everest reached on 29 May by Hillary and Tenzing."

On 31 May Morris rushed on down the valley with his secret news. The coded message was passed to runners who took it to the nearest radio station, where it was transmitted to the British Embassy in Kathmandu. They then sent it to London.

Five thousand miles away, the crowds gathered during the night of 1 June. At dawn the next day, as they waited for the royal procession to make its way through the streets to Westminster Abbey, the newspapers appeared with the great news: "Everest Climbed."

Thomas Hornbein

Reinhold Messner

Junko Tabei

Chris Bonington

Above: Dougal Haston heading towards the Hillary Step. The South Summit is behind him.

NEW DIRECTIONS

"In 1963 the Americans arrived,
determined to go a step further."

Everest CHANGED THE LIVES of all the men who took part in the 1953 expedition.

Suddenly they were famous all over the world and new opportunities arose. In 1955 Charles Evans led the first ascent of Kangchenjunga – the third highest peak in the world – where George Band went to the summit. Hillary and Lowe took part in the first crossing of Antarctica. Westmacott went to the Andes of South America. The Everest reporter, James Morris, became a very successful writer.

Two of the finest climbers, Bourdillon and Noyce, were later killed in the mountains. Some of the team have now died from old age, but several are still alive. Every five years, on 29 May, they meet to celebrate their Everest anniversary at a hotel in North Wales, beneath Mount Snowdon.

Life changed most for Hillary, Hunt and Tenzing. Hunt and Hillary were knighted by the Queen; so the bee-keeper from New Zealand became Sir Edmund Hillary and the army officer became Sir John Hunt. Later Hunt was made a Lord.

Tenzing lived in Darjeeling. As an Indian citizen he could not receive a British knighthood, but he was awarded the George Medal for gallantry. He had no smart clothes for visiting Buckingham Palace to accept the medal, so the Prime Minister of India, Nehru, lent him six of his own suits. Tenzing Norgay – "the Fortunate One" – became a national hero to Indians, Nepalese Sherpas and Tibetans. In the mountains above Darjeeling he founded a national school of mountaineering to train young Indian and Sherpa climbers.

John Hunt became a public servant. He took part in debates at the House of Lords, spoke at endless committee meetings and became president of the Royal Geographical Society. He also organized the Duke of Edinburgh Awards special courses which have now been done by thousands of British schoolchildren. Hunt believed passionately that all young people, particularly those from poor backgrounds, should take part in outdoor adventures.

Edmund Hillary returned countless times to Sola Khumbu, the high valley home of the Sherpas. In 1961 he was there with Griffith Pugh and Michael Ward on a medical research expedition. At the end of the expedition he and some American climbers built a small schoolhouse at the village of Khumjung. It was the first Sherpa school. Since then his Himalayan Trust has helped Sherpas build more schools and hospitals.

As for Everest itself, others soon followed in the steps of Hillary and Tenzing. The Swiss made the second ascent in 1955, as well as making the first ascent of Lhotse. Then in 1963 the Americans arrived, determined to go a step further. The main team repeated the British route from the South Col, with Jim Whittaker becoming the first American to reach the summit. Meanwhile another group took a left turning from the Western Cwm onto the untouched West Ridge. This ridge looked so difficult that they continued left, trespassing into Tibet. They reached a deep gully on the North Face where the Sherpas turned back, leaving Willi Unsoeld and Tom Hornbein perched in a tiny tent.

Hornbein checks out the previously unexplored West Ridge

The next day Unsoeld and Hornbein set off up the gully. The climbing was so hard that they knew they would not be able to return that way. The only way to safety was over the summit and down the South Col route.

The sun was setting when Unsoeld and Hornbein finally saw the American flag on the summit, left three weeks earlier by Whittaker. They also found the faint tracks of Barry Bishop and Lute Jerstad, who had reached the summit by the South Col route earlier that afternoon and were now on their way down. Unsoeld and Hornbein did not have long to enjoy the summit, however. Terrified of being caught by darkness, they hurried down the South-east Ridge, over the Hillary Step and the South Summit.

Bishop and Jerstad knew that their two fellow Americans were in peril somewhere above them and were waiting anxiously for them at the South Summit. It was a wonderful reunion when Unsoeld and Hornbein arrived, and the four climbers tried to continue down to the South Col. Soon it was completely dark. Hornbein was keen to press on anyway, but the others thought it too risky. So, at about 8,300 metres above sea-level, they sat in the snow to wait for dawn. They had no tent or sleeping-bags. It was bitterly cold – at least -30°C – but they were lucky: there was no wind and they survived their night in the open. Just. Unsoeld had such bad frostbite that he later had to have nine toes amputated. Bishop lost all his toes. Hornbein was luckier – and as for his gully on the North Face, it is still known as the Hornbein Couloir.

Like the British and Swiss before them, the Americans relied on the help of the Sherpas. When Whittaker reached the summit he was accompanied by Tenzing's nephew, Nawang Gombu. As a boy, Gombu had been sent to Rongbuk Monastery to become a monk, but he had run away to work for expeditions. In 1953 he had been the youngest Sherpa on the British Everest expedition. Now, in 1963, like his uncle, he reached the summit of Chomolungma. He joined the first Indian ascent of Everest in 1965 and reached the summit again – the first person to do so twice.

Haston on the South-west Face.

Other expeditions followed. Some were successful; many never got to the top. Now that the Americans had found a new route up Everest, people began to wonder about other new routes. During the 1970s several teams tried to climb the great wall rearing straight up out of the Western Cwm – the South-west Face. Time and time again they were defeated.

The South-west Face of Everest became the ultimate goal for high-altitude climbers. Success came finally to a British expedition in the autumn of 1975. The leader was Chris Bonington. Like John Hunt in 1953, he learned the lessons from previous expeditions and left nothing to chance. There were twelve very strong climbers in the team. They were helped by nearly 60 high-altitude Sherpas. Special avalanche-proof tents were bolted onto metal platforms on the face. A continuous

Dougal Haston climbing the Hillary Step, which is covered in monsoon snow

line of rope was fixed all the way up the face, so that climbers could travel safely up and down. Going up they used special clamps called ascenders; going down they abseiled. It was all very different from the very early attempts on the north side of Everest.

The team found a secret gully leading through an immense cliff that had stopped all previous expeditions. Then a tiny tent, Camp VI, was erected above the cliff at 8,200 metres. Doug Scott and Dougal Haston were chosen for the summit. From the tiny tent they had to traverse sideways for about 500 metres, then wade up another gully, piled high with powder snow. At last they stepped out onto the South Summit. All that remained was the famous Hillary Step.

Scott on the summit just after sunset on 24 September 1975

The sun was setting when Haston and Scott reached the summit; they were the first British climbers to get to this magical place. Their oxygen had almost run out and there was no hope of getting back to Camp VI in the dark, so the two men dug a little cave in the snow near the South Summit and crawled inside. All night long they rubbed their feet to keep the circulation going. Amazingly, they escaped without frostbite and returned safely the next morning.

Three days later a second team reached the summit: Peter Boardman and Sherpa Pertemba. On their way back to the South Summit they met Mick Burke coming up towards them. Back in London he worked as a cameraman for the children's programme "Blue Peter". Here, at 8,800 metres, he wanted to film the top of the world. It was late afternoon and cloud was swirling around the summit. It was windy and a storm seemed to be coming. Boardman and Pertemba were anxious to get down but said they would wait for Burke at the South Summit. As they waited, the storm got worse. The wind was blowing snow into their goggles; hands and feet were starting to go numb. If they stayed much longer they would die.

Eventually they had to give up waiting for Mick Burke, who was never seen again. No one knows what happened. Perhaps he stumbled in the storm and slid down the South-west Face. He could have strayed onto one of the deadly snow cornices which jut out over the East Face, which snapped, sending him plunging down the precipice. His body still lies somewhere on Everest.

Nearly 200 people have died on Everest and most of them are still lying on the mountain. A few bodies have been carried down, but moving an adult body is extremely hard work, even at sea-level. At high altitude it is even more difficult, requiring several climbers who need to be breathing bottled oxygen. Most climbers find it hard enough just to get themselves safely down. Generally, if a body is brought down, Sherpas are paid to do the job, as they are usually much stronger than the foreign climbers.

So far in this story there has been hardly any mention of women. In fact, women have climbed mountains ever since the pastime began in the nineteenth century. But for many years no woman was invited on an Everest expedition. Then in the spring of 1975, Junko Tabei, from Japan, became the first woman to reach the summit of Everest. A few days later, climbing from the north side, a Tibetan woman called Phantog also reached the top.

Now many more women have climbed Everest, but the majority of climbers are still men. Obviously women can climb just as well as men: however, they do have some disadvantages. Because men are generally bigger, it is easier for them to carry heavy loads. Then there is the tiresome business of having a pee, when the last thing you want to do is crawl out of your tent into a blizzard. The answer is to use a pee bottle – easy for men, but not so easy for women. (As for having a poo, you have to go outside for that, and it isn't much fun. It's important to have zips on all your layers of clothing.)

Perhaps the hardest part of an expedition is being away from home for several weeks. For climbers who have children, this can be very hard. For some reason people think it is worse for mothers to be away from their children than fathers. Nevertheless, parents do manage to cope with the absence. For instance, Marija Stremfelj and her husband Andrej from Slovenia left their children with her sister when they went to climb Everest in 1990. And in doing so became the first married couple to reach the top of the world.

Over a thousand people have now reached the summit of Everest. Nearly all of them have used bottled oxygen to help them climb into the very thin air at 8,800 metres. After the success of the 1953 expedition, which used oxygen, people assumed that it must be necessary. However, one climber believed it must be possible to climb without it.

Reinhold Messner grew up in the Dolomite mountains, in northern Italy. He started climbing with his father, brothers and sisters when he was a boy. By the age of 25 he was one of the best climbers in the world and he started to climb some of the highest Himalayan peaks. One of them, in northern Pakistan, was called Hidden Peak – one of only 14 summits over 8,000 metres. Rather than use a team of porters to help him, Messner decided to do things differently. With just one partner, Peter Habeler, he climbed straight up the mountain in two days, and descended on the third day.

After their success on Hidden Peak, Messner and Habeler decided to try Everest without oxygen. There was still only one expedition allowed on the mountain per year and the mountain was booked up ten years in advance. The only way to get there was to join a large Austrian–German expedition with a permit for spring 1978. Habeler and Messner climbed separately, eventually reaching the South Col. On 10 May 1978, they set off up the South-east Ridge – the route of Hillary and Tenzing.

Ten hours later they arrived, exhausted, on the summit of Everest. They had proved Everest could be climbed without artificial help.

You would think that Messner would be satisfied with that achievement. But he was planning even bolder feats. He was looking, in particular, to the other side of Everest – to Tibet. Ever since 1950 Tibet had been occupied by Chinese troops. No foreigners had been allowed

Messner (left) and Habeler relax before their historic climb

across the border; the north and east sides of Everest were out of bounds. But Chinese climbers did visit Rongbuk. In 1960 they even built a road all the way to the old British Base Camp, and that year they succeeded in climbing the old British northern route. Not everyone in the west believed them. However, we do know for certain that Chinese and Tibetan climbers, including the woman climber Phantog, reached the top in 1975, because they left a metal tripod on the summit.

In 1980 the Chinese government announced that foreigners could now visit Tibet, so now there could be visits on both sides of the mountain. That spring a Japanese team arrived at Rongbuk, to climb the old British route and also a new route up the North Face. Then, when they had all gone home, Reinhold Messner arrived.

Messner did not come with a great expedition. His only companions were his girlfriend, Nena Holguin, two Chinese government officials, and a few yaks to carry luggage to his camp beneath the North Col. Above this "Advance Base" he would be completely alone.

His only hope of success was to get very well acclimatized. So for nearly a month he went for long walks, exploring the countryside and visiting Tibetan nomads at their camps. Then he returned to Advance Base. He left at night, climbing steep snow and ice to the North Col. He continued up the North Ridge before stopping to pitch his tiny, lightweight nylon tent, which weighed just two kilograms. The next day, carrying everything he needed in his rucksack, he traversed to the right across the North Face. It was August and Everest was smothered in monsoon snow. At times Messner was sinking in up to his knees. But he ploughed on. He stopped to camp a second time, close to the Great Couloir. The next morning he left the tent where it was and headed across the Couloir. He climbed out on the far side, somewhere near where Edward Norton had turned back in 1924. It was cloudy and he could hardly see

73

where he was going, but some instinct helped him to find his way through rocky cliffs. At 1.00 p.m. he fell to his knees beside the Chinese tripod on the summit. He was utterly alone at the top of the world.

When he got back to his tent, Messner was too weak to light the stove and melt snow. The next day, he knew his only chance of survival was to leave everything behind, as he felt too weak to carry his equipment. It was a desperate gamble but it worked. That evening, four days after setting out, he was back at the foot of the mountain.

Messner's solo ascent of Everest in 1980 showed what was possible. It inspired others to go further into the unknown, and to explore new routes with less

Reinhold Messner rests on the summit next to the Chinese tripod

and less equipment. Messner had kept alight the flame of adventure.

An Australian team led by Tim Macartney-Snape, also managing without oxygen, climbed a new route, straight up the Great Couloir. Two Swiss climbers, Erhard Loretan and Jean Troillet, astounded the world when they climbed the North Face, up and down, in just 43 hours. To avoid carrying tents and sleeping-bags, they climbed at night and rested during the day, when it was a little warmer. Nothing like that was possible for the Polish team that made the first winter ascent of Everest. For them, the only hope of success was to work away at the mountain, week by week, building secure camps and fixing ropes to stop the vicious winter winds blowing them off the mountain. When Leszek Cichy and Krzystof Wielicki eventually reached the summit, the temperature was about -50°C.

One of the most exciting new climbs on Everest was the East Face, also known as the Kangshung Face. Mallory had looked at it in 1921 and decided it looked crazy. But with modern equipment and skills, perhaps it would be possible. In 1983 an American expedition succeeded in climbing this face. Their route was one of the hardest that had ever been done on Everest. They had a large team and the five summit climbers all used oxygen.

No foreigner visited the Kangshung Face for five years. Then in 1988 I arrived there with Robert Anderson, Paul Teare and Ed Webster. We wanted to see whether we could find another new route up the Kangshung Face. Just four of us. Without oxygen.

The author at dawn in Tibet. Everest is in the distance, to the left of his head.

Right: Robert Anderson climbing a fixed rope up the ice towers of the East Face. The Kangshung Glacier is 1,000 metres below him.

Welcome The Mountaineers From Three Countries

雄的三国登山健儿！

Above: from left Ed Webster (USA), Stephen Venables (Britain), Robert Anderson (USA) and Paul Teare (Canada).

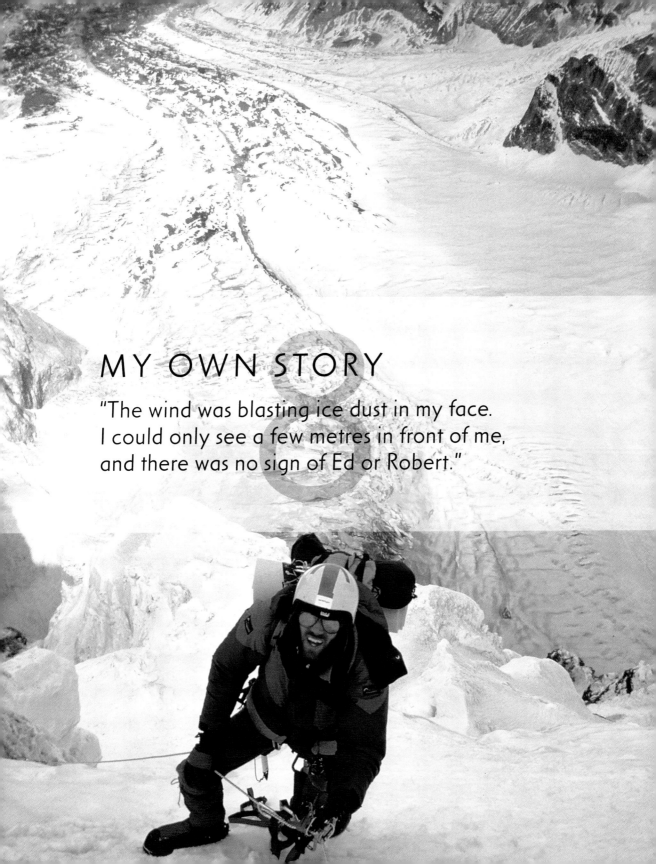

MY OWN STORY

"The wind was blasting ice dust in my face.
I could only see a few metres in front of me,
and there was no sign of Ed or Robert."

People OFTEN ASK ME how to train for Everest. I always

reply that the best training is to go and climb lots of other mountains first. When we went to Everest in 1988 each of us had been climbing for about fifteen years, and it was my tenth Himalayan expedition. But as well as experience, you need to have the right attitude. You need determination and patience; and you also have to remember that, in the end, a lot will depend on luck.

You also need time. We were away for four months. Because deep snow was blocking the high passes, it took nearly three weeks just to walk from the end of the road to Base Camp. It was hard for us, but a lot tougher for the Tibetan porters carrying all the luggage.

Some of the 100 porters carry expedition supplies and equipment to Base Camp

Eventually we reached the high meadow in the Kama valley which would be our home for the next two months – Base Camp. The porters were paid and returned to their villages. That left Ed, Paul, Robert and me. Looking after Base Camp there was also Mimi Zieman, our doctor; Joe Blackburn, the photographer; Pasang Norbu, an old Sherpa friend of Ed's who was the expedition cook; and a young Tibetan man called Kasang Tsering to help Pasang.

This group – seven men and one woman – became almost like a family, isolated from the rest of the world. Nowadays most expeditions have satellite telephones; in 1988 we were cut off from the outside. But we had everything we needed, including all our food. Much of it had been shipped from America, but Pasang had

organized all the basics – such as rice, potatoes, onions, vegetables, spices, garlic, oil, sugar, and flour for making bread and chapattis – in Kathmandu. At Base Camp we had three cooked meals a day. At Advance Base, on the glacier, things were a bit simpler. On the mountain itself everything had to be made with melted snow, so we kept meals very simple. The most important thing high up was to get as much liquid as possible.

During seven weeks on Everest, I only climbed on 25 days. Other days were spent resting in the valley, often waiting for the weather to improve. I loved rest days – reading, chatting, sleeping and eating large meals. But in between we worked very hard indeed.

The work was fun, because we were exploring. No human being had ever touched the rock, snow and ice where we made our route day by day. Because the climbing was very steep and complicated, we sometimes only made about 300 metres in a day. So we left ropes in place, allowing us to abseil down to the reasonably comfortable Advance Base Camp and come back up the next day. The scenery was incredible and we found ourselves in amazing places. There were immense striped walls of rock. Huge snow gullies. And an incredible ridge of gleaming ice towers, like giant crystal vegetables, which we called the Cauliflower Towers. It was here, 1,000 metres up the

Top: two figures at work on the Cauliflower Towers, 1,000 metres up the Kangshung Face

Bottom: the author carrying supplies

79

...Kangshung Face, that we were stopped dead by a huge crevasse.

Paul and I carried up supplies for a camp on the towers, Camp I. In the meantime, Ed and Robert sorted out the crevasse. We had no ladders, so Ed and Robert slid down a rope into the bottom of the ice chasm. Then Ed climbed 30 metres up the far wall. It was vertical – no more than vertical: actually overhanging. But with modern ice axes and crampons he was able to work his way up the smooth wall of ice. Once Ed reached the top of the far wall, he was able to pull a rope tight and create a bridge over the crevasse. That opened the way to the summit.

All this activity took place over days and weeks, but eventually we were ready to try for the top. I can still remember the last evening at Camp I, wondering if I was going to be strong enough. Wondering if the weather would stay fine, but not daring to hope too much, knowing that we still had such a long way to go.

The move from Camp I to Camp II took 14 hours. Then the third day felt even harder. Without any Sherpas helping, we were carrying everything on our own backs. In the morning it was so hot, even at 7,600 metres, that we wore just our long underwear; by the end of the day I had on five layers of clothing. It was almost dark when we staggered out onto the flat surface of the South Col. We were the first people ever to get there from Tibet.

We had reached the point described at the beginning of this book. In the morning Paul, after all the weeks of work, felt unwell and decided to descend. Before he left, he shouted into the wind, "Get to the top. Make me proud." It was that night that we left for the summit.

Soon after leaving the South Col, we decided to unrope, so that each person could move at his own speed, following his own rhythm. Although a rope can give you security, it requires great skill to hold a falling climber if you are moving together. At that altitude, climbing without oxygen, we felt that we just didn't have that skill. In fact, most summit parties on Everest these days climb unroped.

I went ahead, making tracks in the snow. But I could see Ed's and Robert's torch lights below. After about four hours the blackness faded to grey. Then there was a glorious explosion of light and colour as the sun rose in the east. Far below us summits of other famous mountains in Nepal glowed peachy orange. The world seemed a beautiful place again.

We had hoped to reach the summit in about twelve hours (Messner and Habeler had managed in ten), but it was proving desperately hard. Twelve hours passed and I had still not reached the South Summit. I was having to stop and rest every step. Eventually I just slumped in the snow and dozed for an hour. Then Ed appeared a short way below me. He was barely moving. Robert was even further behind. Our expedition seemed to be falling to pieces.

It was then that I decided to make one final effort. After a swig of juice from my half-frozen water bottle, I stood up and continued. I forced my legs to kick into the snow – left – breathe, right – breathe, left – breathe... I forced myself to do at least five steps before stopping to rest. I seemed to be in charge of my body again, driving it up the steep slope towards the South Summit.

At 1.30 p.m. I reached the South Summit. And there was the final ridge just in front of me. This was where Bourdillon and Evans had made their decision to turn back in 1953.

For me it was easier. I knew the Hillary Step was possible and that from there it was less than 500 horizontal metres to the summit. There were still a few hours of daylight left, so I decided to continue.

A big part of the thrill of climbing Everest is following in the steps of the great pioneers. You almost feel as though you are stepping back in history. It was very moving to reach the final obstacle – that 18-metre-high cliff first climbed by Hillary and Tenzing. Like them – and the many other climbers who have repeated their route – I could feel the immense drop into

Early morning – Webster and Teare above the steepest part of the climb after leaving Camp 1

space, just a few inches from my nose. There is usually a rope on the Step these days, so you can clip in for safety. That makes a huge difference.

Beyond the Hillary Step, it is just a case of putting one foot in front of the other. Plod, plod, plod, step by step, over three or four snowy hummocks, until at last you stagger up one final hummock and, suddenly, find yourself staring down the North Face. There is nowhere further to go.

The Hillary Step

My only regret was that Ed and Robert had not made it this far. Later I heard that they were forced to turn back at the South Summit, which they reached just before dark. Alone on the summit, I had one task to do. Two Indian friends, Nawang and Sonam, both named after famous Sherpas, had given me a small gift for the summit. Deep inside one of my pockets I had two little envelopes containing holy flower petals from a religious centre in India. I took out Sonam's and Nawang's envelopes, scattered the petals on the snow and left the envelopes beside three empty oxygen cylinders which were sitting on the summit.

Then it was time to leave. It was 3.40 p.m. and in three hours it would be dark. The summit of Everest is a very dangerous place to be without oxygen equipment, especially if you are alone. As soon as I started down, I realized just how tired I was. Several times I had to stop and kneel in the snow to get my breath back. At the bottom of the Hillary Step I had to take off my prescription sunglasses because they were covered in ice. Then in order to get my regular glasses out of a pocket, I had to take off one mitten. As I fumbled in the pocket I felt the cold searing my fingers through my thin inner gloves. Terrified of frostbite

The abandoned tent where Webster and Anderson sheltered overnight

I decided to forget about the glasses and somehow manage without, in spite of being very shortsighted. Then I had a desperate struggle to get the mittens back on. Peering through the murk, I continued along the ridge towards the South Summit. Snow was falling, filling up my tracks from the way up and the wind was blasting ice dust in my face. I could only see a few metres in front of me, and there was no sign of Ed or Robert. No one was going to get me out of this fix – it was up to me to cope on my own.

Determined to return home, I forced myself back over the South Summit and continued down towards the South Col. But I was too slow. Night was falling and I dared not risk making a mistake in the dark. I stopped to cut a ledge in the snow, and lay down to wait for the dawn. The storm had blown over, thank goodness, but it was still going to be a long, hard night.

That night passed in a strange, confused blur. Hour after hour I lay in the snow, shivering and dreaming of warm places. My brain, starved of oxygen, kept imagining that other people were there with me: an old man helping keep my hands warm; another person trying to warm my feet, unsuccessfully. At one point I imagined it was Eric Shipton; some Tibetan yak-herders invited me to go and sit by their fire. Someone even offered me a hot bath.

Every once in a while I would suddenly realize where I was, completely alone, higher than any other human being on earth. No one had ever brought yaks up here and Eric Shipton had been dead for twelve years. In these returns to reality, I did what I could to look after myself. I wriggled my fingers inside my mittens. I sat up and stamped my feet to try and improve circulation. I even made the effort to reach into a deep pocket and take out the remains of a bar of chocolate. It tasted like cardboard, but it would give me a few extra calories to fight the cold.

I think I fell asleep for a short while; then I realized, joyfully, that it was no longer dark. Once again, the daily miracle of sunrise had brought light and colour. And a glimmer of warmth. I was alive and soon I would be back with my friends!

I found Ed and Robert in an old abandoned tent, a few hundred metres lower down. They too had failed to get back before dark and had crawled in here to shelter. About once every hour, during the night, Robert had asked to set off down for the South Col, and each time Ed had insisted that they had to wait until dawn. Now the three of us did finally set off down to the South Col and our own tents.

We had always known that Everest without oxygen would be very, very hard. It turned out to be even harder than we expected. After our night out without

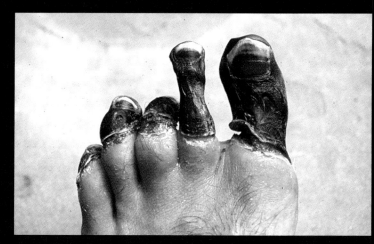

The author's frostbitten toes three months after the ascent

sleeping-bags, all of us had some frostbite. Later, poor Ed was to lose the tips of seven fingers and a thumb. Robert only lost a bit of flesh off the tips of two toes and a couple of fingers, but I lost three and a half toes on my left foot.

In our weak state it took us another three days to descend the East Face, and we only reached the safety of the Advance Base nine days after setting out for the summit. We were in a mess, but Paul, Mimi, Joe, Pasang and Kasang were there to pick up the pieces. And none of us regretted our great adventure on Everest.

Leo Dickinson's stunning view along the Nepal–Tibet border. The East Face of Everest is on the left.

EXTRAORDINARY FEATS

"…we go to the mountains because they are places of peace and beauty."

In 1988 ROBERT, ED, PAUL AND I had our chance to

write our own chapter in Everest's history. Of course the story has continued since then. I was the 203rd person to reach the summit; now it has been reached by over a thousand people. One man, Sherpa Apa, has been to the top twelve times.

Extraordinary feats have been achieved. In 1999 Sherpa Babu Chiri raced up the 1953 route, all the way from Base Camp to the summit, in just sixteen hours – as long as it took me just to get from the South Col. Everest has now been jumped off with a paraglider; skied down; and, most incredible of all, snowboarded down! The snowboarder, Marco Siffredi, with help from Lobsang Temba carrying equipment on the way up, slid down the North Face, starting off down the same terrifying bank of the Great Couloir that Norton had tried to climb up 77 years earlier. Perhaps the most risky feat of all was the first balloon crossing of Everest in 1991. It was possible only with the help of satellite communications, and getting detailed weather forecasts from one of the world's top forecasting stations in Britain. Even then the balloonists were at the mercy of 160 kph winds, as they blasted through

the upper atmosphere at about 9,000 metres. Each man wore a parachute in case he had to bail out in an emergency. In the end they crash-landed on the Tibetan Plateau, but before crashing to earth, Leo Dickinson took some magnificent photos of Everest.

Nowadays there are more women climbers on the mountain. Stacy Allison became the first American woman to reach the summit in 1988; Rebecca Stephens was the first British

Alison Hargreaves

Leo Dickinson stares into his own remote controlled camera from his balloon, flying at 160 kph over Everest, which is on the left edge of the photo

---

woman in 1993. But the most impressive was Alison Hargreaves. In 1995 she climbed the northern route up Everest, carrying her own tent, making her own camps, and reaching the summit without oxygen. It was a terrible tragedy when she was killed three months later, 1,300 kilometres away from Everest, on her way down from the summit of K2.

Since we climbed our route up the East Face, other new routes have been climbed on Everest. The hardest was probably the long Northeast Ridge. But most of the hundreds of climbers have stuck to the old North Col route from Tibet and the Western Cwm/South Col route from Nepal. Nowadays, in the busy spring season, 30 or more climbers can arrive on the summit on a single day.

You might wonder why so many people seem to find it so easy these days. The answer is that it is not easy, even with oxygen equipment. Everest will always be very hard work and quite dangerous.

But nowadays the governments of Nepal and Tibet allow many more teams to visit the mountain each year. And the odds are now much more in favour of the climbers. They are helped by accurate weather forecasts received by satellite telephone, fax and e-mail. Tents are lighter and easier to pitch. Very strong, lightweight ropes are made out of Kevlar. Clothing is generally better. Plastic boots are much lighter on the feet than the old leather boots. Modern crampons allow you to move more quickly and confidently on ice. Stoves are easier to cook on. The oxygen equipment has become more reliable and much lighter. But perhaps the biggest change is that most climbers now arrive at the mountain with commercial organized expeditions. The organizers are usually American or European, but much of the work is done by Sherpas. In 1953 it was the foreigners who were in charge, these days most of the leading is done by the Sherpas. They fix ropes and ladders, pitch the camps and carry spare oxygen. They provide a very efficient guiding service.

Rubbish, including empty oxygen cylinders, dumped at the South Col

Despite all this, things can still easily go wrong. In 1996 several teams were caught by a storm near the summit and a number of people died. The dead included the guides Rob Fischer, who collapsed and froze to death, and Rob Hall, who stayed up near the South Summit when his client, Doug Hanson, became too weak to move. During the night Hanson either died or fell off the mountain – no one discovered exactly what happened – and by the morning Hall was too cold and too weak to move. His Sherpa friends tried heroically to climb up the South Col with fresh supplies of oxygen and hot drinks, but they were knocked back by the icy winds. Later that day Hall made his final radio call, and soon after became unconscious. His dead body was found at the South Summit by another party a week later. Altogether, eight people died during that storm in 1996. It was a cruel reminder that no one can guarantee total safety on any high mountain.

With all this activity, Everest has become very crowded on the two main routes. Because most foreigners are not strong enough or are just too lazy to carry down all their equipment and empty oxygen cylinders, a lot of rubbish has been left on the mountain. Journalists write about this in the newspapers – in fact they have become completely obsessed with rubbish. My own feeling is that the whole thing has become exaggerated. I hate to see rubbish lying around too, but the world has more important problems to think about. Nevertheless, we go to the mountains because they are places of peace and beauty. And no one likes to camp on a rubbish-tip. So nowadays, Sherpas – stronger than most of us – are being paid to carry down old equipment and packaging. Things are improving a bit.

With all those crowds, many mountaineers prefer not to go to Everest. The world is full of fantastic rock walls and mountains, not to mention the great ice sheets of Greenland and Antarctica. Every continent has so much to explore. In Asia alone there are thousands and thousands of mountains, many of them steeper, more challenging and more beautiful than Everest. What is important for us the visitors is to treat those mountains with respect. After all, for millions of people who live in the shadow of the Himalaya, those mountains are holy places. And they are the source of life for millions. If you take the Himalaya to include all the complicated ranges at the western and eastern ends, then if you look at all the great rivers which start amongst the snows of those mountains, you will see how vital they are. Most of China and India – nearly half the world's population – get their water supply from these mountains.

Many centuries ago, one of the ancient Hindu sages wrote: "In a thousand ages of the gods I could not tell you of all the glories of the Himalaya." Even today, when every peak, glacier and valley of the immense range can be photographed from space satellites, it is still a source of wonder. Everest itself, despite all the people who tramp up and down its slopes, remains an object of wonder and fascination. For that great pyramid at the heart of Asia will always remain the highest spot on earth.

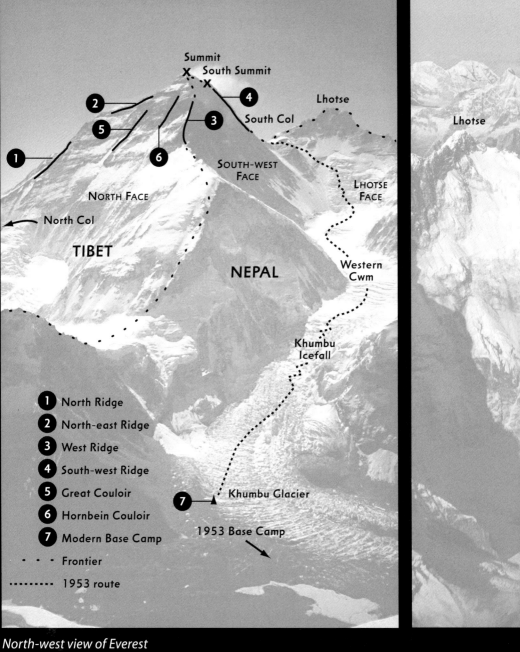

Summit
X
South Summit
X

Lhotse

2

5

1

6

4

South Col

3

SOUTH-WEST
FACE

Lhotse

NORTH FACE

LHOTSE
FACE

North Col

Western
Cwm

TIBET

NEPAL

Khumbu
Icefall

1 North Ridge

2 North-east Ridge

3 West Ridge

4 South-west Ridge

5 Great Couloir

7

Khumbu Glacier

6 Hornbein Couloir

7 Modern Base Camp

1953 Base Camp

• • • Frontier

• • • • 1953 route

North-west view of Everest
showing 1953 route

East view of Everest showing 1988 route

Within the image:

Summit **X**
South Summit **X**
3
2
1
th Col
6
EAST FACE
5
4

1 South-east Ridge
2 North-east Ridge
3 Hillary and Tenzing's final camp 1953
4 Camp 1 1988
5 Camp 2 1988
6 Camp 3 1988
········ 1988 route

ngshung lacier

ALTITUDE SICKNESS – dizziness, nausea, loss of concentration and balance, and possible hallucinations caused by the lack of oxygen at high altitudes. Extreme altitude sickness can also lead to pulmonary oedema (water on the lungs) or cerebral oedema (water on the brain), which can lead quickly to death unless treated by rapid evacuation to lower altitude.

BASE CAMP – an expedition's headquarters, usually at the foot of the mountain.

CHIMNEY – a narrow, vertical channel in rock or ice.

COL – a hollow in a mountain range, similar to a pass, but not necessarily able to be crossed.

COULOIR – a gully filled with snow or ice.

CRAMPON – a metal frame fitted with spikes which is attached to the sole of the boot. Used for climbing on hard snow and ice.

CREVASSE – a deep split in a glacier.

CWM – a bowl-shaped valley enclosed by high mountain walls.

FACE – the surface of the mountain between ridges.

FROSTBITE – when the blood stops reaching parts of the body (usually fingers and toes) due to the severe cold. The flesh becomes frozen and can, in severe cases, rot away.

GLACIER – a slow-moving river of ice fed by snow at higher altitudes.

GULLY – a channel in the rock, often formed by running water. The English word for couloir.

ICE FALL – a broken part of a glacier, often formed as the glacier changes direction or steepens.

ICE TOWER – a huge block of ice.

MONSOON – the season of subtropical winds that bring rain to the Indian subcontinent, and snow higher up in the Himalaya, between late May and late September.

PASS – a dip on a high mountain ridge, where it is possible to cross from one side of the mountain – or a whole mountain range – to another.

SADDLE – see col.

SIRDAR – the head Sherpa.

SNOW-BLINDNESS – a temporary but painful condition caused by the harsh, bright light reflecting off snow.

SNOWFIELD – a wide stretch or expanse of snow.

93

ROYAL GEOGRAPHICAL SOCIETY
WITH THE INSTITUTE OF BRITISH GEOGRAPHERS

The SOCIETY WAS FOUNDED in 1830 and given a Royal Charter in 1859 for "the advancement of geographical science". It was pivotal in establishing geography as a teaching and research discipline in British universities and has played a key role in geographical and environmental education ever since. The Society holds historical collections of national and international importance, many of which relate to its association with and support for scientific exploration and research from the nineteenth century onwards.

Today the Society is a leading world centre for geographical learning – supporting education, teaching, research and expeditions, as well as promoting public understanding and enjoyment of the subject.

The Society welcomes those interested in geography as members. For further information, please visit the website: www.rgs.org

The Royal Geographical Society Picture Library holds within its collection a unique international photographic resource on the subject of Everest. The images forming the Everest Archive were all taken on the Mount Everest expeditions of 1921, 1922, 1924, 1933, 1935, 1936, 1938, 1951 and the successful expedition of 1953. The Society would like to thank Rolex for its generous support of the Everest Archive Project 2001–2003. This support has allowed photographs taken on the nine British Mount Everest expeditions to be catalogued and electronically databased. This important information will be available online and widely accessible.

The Mount Everest Foundation, formed by the Society and the Alpine Club, continues to support the exploration and understanding of the world's mountain regions. Over 1,300 expeditions have received grants since 1953. Further details of MEF and the plans to celebrate the 50th anniversary of the first ascent of Everest can be found on the websites www.mef.org.uk and www.rgs.org/Everest50